4/93

Laine, Frankie,
1913-

That lucky old son.

3 02/10
last one

DATE			

THAT LUCKY OLD SON
THE AUTOBIOGRAPHY OF FRANKIE LAINE

THAT LUCKY OLD SON
THE AUTOBIOGRAPHY OF FRANKIE LAINE

By

FRANKIE LAINE
and
JOSEPH F. LAREDO

Pathfinder Publishing of California

Ventura, CA

THAT LUCKY OLD SON:

The Autobiography of Frankie Laine

by

Frankie Laine and Joseph F. Laredo

Published By:
Pathfinder Publishing of California
458 Dorothy Avenue
Ventura, CA 93003
(805) 642-9278

Copyright © 1993 by Frankie Laine & Joseph F. Laredo

Library of Congress Cataloging-in-Publication Data

Laine, Frankie, 1913-
    That lucky old son : the autobiography of Frankie Laine / by
Franke Laine and Joseph F. Laredo.
        p.   cm.
    Discography: p.
    Includes index.
    ISBN)-934793-45-X : $21.95. -- ISBN 0-934793-46-8 (pbk) : $14.95
    1. Laine, Frankie, 1913- . 2. Singers--United States-
-Biography. I. Laredo, Joseph F., 1964- . II. Title.
ML420.L224A3   1993
782.42164'092--dc20
[B]   92-29071
                                                      CIP
                                                       MN

DEDICATIONS

In fond memory of CARL FISCHER, AL JARVIS, and HOAGY CARMICHAEL. Without those guys, there might not have been much of a career to write about.

And most especially for my beloved wife NAN, who has provided both this book and my life with a "happy ending" that I hope never ends.

Frankie Laine

To my mother, for everything.

J.F.L.

ACKNOWLEDGEMENTS

The authors would like to express their sincere gratitude to the following:

Muriel Moore, Mr. Laine's loyal secretary since 1948.

All of those who have worked so hard on behalf of the Frankie Laine Society of America, including: Vicky and Soddy Lorand, Helen Snow, Don Dyck, John Lambrosa, and many others.

The faithful and resourceful members of the Frankie Laine International Appreciation Society, among them: Ron and Rosemary Carden, Paul Durham, Alan and Jean Inns, Dr. Mac Robinson, Tony Cooper, Bert Boorman (who, along with Don Champeny of the FLSOA, is a discographer par excellence), and others.

Thanks also to: Berle Adams, Sam Lutz, Henry Miller, and Ken Hart.

For their kind words: Tony Bennett, Mitch Miller, Patti Page, Joe Smith, Jo Stafford, Kay Starr, and Paul Weston.

A special word of gratitude to the late Irving Stone, as well as Mrs. Stone and his family.

Mr. Laine would also like to extend his appreciation to Hal Shaper of the Sparta Florida Music Group Limited. Mr. Shaper worked wonders in straightening out the publishing affairs of Cares Music in Britain, and he was invaluable in securing (for re-release) the masters of the two Laine albums recorded for Polydor. His continued friendship is valued very highly.

Finally, the authors would like to thank our publisher, Eugene D. Wheeler, and the staff of Pathfinder Publishing for all of their help and enthusiastic belief in this book.

PRELUDE

by

IRVING STONE

Frankie Laine is my favorite among the contemporary singers of popular songs.

Why? Well, these things are purely personal, don't you think? What moves me may not move you. Each person has a certain style and area of contemporary music which he prefers to others. But there are aspects of Frankie's singing that have meant a great deal to me over the years, and I would like to tell you about a few of them.

Firstly, Frankie is never impersonal. He does not sing to an audience. He sings to me. I feel that he is communicating with me, that there are only the two of us in all the world. In short, he is able to create a **rapport,** an atmosphere of two friends alone in a room, the one singing to the other.

Secondly, Frankie knows precisely what it is he wants to say through a song. He does not mouth words or belt out phrases that he does not understand. What he sings, he feels; that is why he is able to make the listener feel the same emotion.

All of which leads me to my perhaps most important point. Frankie loves to sing, better than anything else in the world. He has been singing since he was a kid in a Chicago church choir. He enjoys himself so hugely while he is singing that the listener is swept up in a contagious enthusiasm. He never gives one whit less than the utmost of his vitality, his dedication to music, and his natural talent. As a result, our own enjoyment is considerably heightened. Frankie's powerful male voice gets under our skin. Some few might not like it, but be indifferent? Never.

One anecdote should sum up the story. Mrs. Stone and I were living in Rome when an evening concert by the American singer, Frankie Laine, was announced in the Italian press. An enormous movie house, seating perhaps 2,000, was taken over for the evening. My wife and I went early. . . and were disappointed to find the lower floor almost empty. But by ten o'clock, when the mediocre vaudeville acts were over and Frankie was to make his appearance, the house was packed. At one o'clock in the morning not a soul had left the theater, and Frankie was going strong on his twentieth encore. When he had finally finished, the audience stood and cheered.

Why? For that audience as for me, the feeling was that Frankie was singing to each one of them, personally. That he knew what he was singing, and felt deeply the lyrics and music. So did each and every listener.

That's why the audience, a cross-cut of every age and income level of Rome, gave Frankie Laine his well-earned ovation.

Irving Stone

(The late Mr. Stone, best-selling author of *The Agony and the Ecstasy*, *Lust for Life*, and numerous other classic biographical novels, originally wrote this piece for his friend Frankie Laine as an introduction to the 1962 Columbia album, *Deuces Wild*.)

TABLE OF CONTENTS

PREFACE

This is the story of the way things have gone for me these past eighty years.

I've tried to remember the good times and the hard times with accuracy and honesty. We're all muddling through life for a reason, unclear as it sometimes may be, and the highs and lows of experience are just two different sides of the same spinning coin. In the end all that really matters is the effort you make to do the most with your particular place in time.

I believe in helping others along the way, and you have to truly know yourself before you can do that well. By putting down this story I've come to know myself a little better, and I hope that through reading it others might be inspired to follow their own dreams and aspirations. There are no guarantees and it's not always easy, but you won't be able to live with yourself unless you know you tried.

Many people have had smoother trips through life, and a lot more have endured rockier ones. This is just a description of the route I took. I hope it brings you a little enjoyment.

Frankie Laine
San Diego, California
1992

PROLOGUE

A NEW BEGINNING

On January 16, 1985, my wife Nan and I were busy moving into our new "dream house" in San Diego. It was a welcoming, comfortable place done with a nautical motif, exactly the sort of home we had talked about since moving to this lovely city in 1968. We'd finally found the perfect plot of land, and the ground was broken on June 15, 1983, our 33rd wedding anniversary. Nan had worked closely with the architects and the result was a beautiful, two-story structure high on a sandstone hill with a panoramic view of the Pacific, the San Diego Harbor, and the Coronado Islands. On clear days, I could even make out a bullring on the Baja Peninsula! After 54 years as a professional singer and a hell of a lot of time on the road, I finally had a little piece of paradise to come home to. I told friends that I'd part with the house for nothing, but any buyer would have to come up with ten million dollars for the setting.

I'd been experiencing chest pains recently, so I kept to the sidelines and left the heavy stuff to the movers. I tried to pitch in by sitting on a wooden crate and checking off

1

the items as they were unloaded. It took a couple of days to get everything indoors, and by the time the movers drove away I felt rested enough to begin some light unpacking.

On January 22, I came across a big box that contained two large paintings. I didn't feel up to lifting anything that size, so I laid it on its side and began to slide out the contents when I felt a searing burst of pain. I decided that those paintings could just stay put for the time being, took a nitroglycerin tablet, and quit for the day.

In the early hours of the following morning, the pain came back. At 1:30 it woke me up and I took a nitro again. Ninety minutes later things were worse, so I took another pill. By this time I'd awakened Nan. She sat up in bed and looked me over with concern. When I felt the need for a third pill at 4:30, she refused to go back to sleep and insisted on watching over me until I settled into a fitful rest.

After we got up I felt fine and was sure that the trouble, whatever the cause, had straightened itself out. I had a doctor's appointment later that morning anyway, so rather than sit around and worry I tried to put the tossing and turning out of my mind until I could describe my symptoms and get a professional opinion. It seemed like a good idea to get some fresh air and take our little black poodle, Monsieur Noir, out for his morning walk. The moment I took my first uphill step, the pain returned. I looked into his disappointed eyes and cut the walk short, returning home to spend an edgy and uncomfortable hour staring at the clock before leaving for my doctor's appointment.

When I arrived and described my troubles to Dr. Cummins, he advised me to cancel all travel plans for the next few days. I was scheduled to leave later that afternoon for a Meals-on-Wheels benefit performance in Concord, California, and to fly on from there to Edmonton, Alberta,

Canada, for a two-day telethon. Instead, I was given an EKG and told to pack a few things in a bag and drive myself to the hospital.

At Mercy Hospital Dr. John Mazur scheduled an angiogram for the following morning that uncovered the problem. I had "significant blockage in my left ventricle," which when translated meant that only about 5% of the proper blood flow was getting through. They were going to operate.

I tried taking this in stride and asked him when he was going to schedule the surgery, counting on at least a week or two to get things in order. When he shot back "Tomorrow morning!" my eyes widened. I hadn't really grasped the urgency of my situation until that moment. Now I had an uncomfortable feeling that the events of the past few days were snowballing into something ominous.

The next morning, January 25, Nan came to the hospital and spent eight long hours in the waiting room before the doctors came out to assure her that the operation was a success. Dr. Houseman and his team felt secure they'd put in a good day's work. Since there was nothing she could do and I was still groggy from the anesthetic, they urged Nan to go home and rest. Then someone on the staff tried to rouse me a little to check and see that everything was all right.

I was still hooked up to the respirator, but I remember opening my eyes and thinking that I sure felt lousy after an operation that was supposed to improve the state of my health. In another minute I lost consciousness. This time, I came very close to never waking up again.

Something was wrong with the pacemaker that had been stitched onto the outside of my body. Suddenly I went into cardiac arrest and for ten seconds there were no vital signs and, essentially, no more Frankie Laine. The attending physician, Dr. Virgilio, immediately cut me open and

3

began massaging my heart with his hand. He was still at it 45 minutes later. Poor Nan, who had called the hospital for some reassuring words, was instead told to get herself down there right away. The situation was *very* serious.

While all this was going on, my mind was a merciful blank. I think, however, that if I could somehow have been standing at the side of the operating table, looking on as a surgeon literally held my life in the palm of his hand while harshly whispering "Come back to me, damn it!" under his breath, that I would have filled in the blank with thoughts of different rooms and different times. So many memories. I would have thought about family life in Chicago's Little Italy and the affection with which my friends used to holler my nickname, "Spaghett." I would have remembered the early morning chill in New York years later when the only bed I could afford was a splintered bench in Central Park. I would have rejoiced in all the happiness that my beloved wife has brought into my life.

Then I might have cried at the thought of never singing another song. Our new castle on a hill could so easily transform into an empty, miserable dungeon for a grieving widow. God knows that I've been blessed with my fair share of luck, but how could it run out now, on the brink of a new home and a different way of life? There was so much more I wanted to do. . . .

ONE

AN OLD BLUES RECORD

After giving it a lot of thought, I've come to the sad conclusion that the very first thing I can remember is Pa holding me above my baby sister Rose's funeral casket so I could kiss her goodbye. This was in 1917. I was four years old and she was two. We had both come down with a bad case of diphtheria, and poor little Rose didn't make it. There's an old Italian superstition that something bad will happen to someone if their picture falls off a wall, and Rose's baby portrait came crashing off its peg in the hallway shortly before she died. It was a cruel blow for a family that knew hard times all too well.

I was the oldest of eight children, born Francesco Paolo LoVecchio on March 30, 1913, in the Little Italy section of Chicago. Rose was next, then came my little brothers Sam, Joe, John, another daughter my parents also named Rose, Gloria, and the baby of the bunch, Phil. I guess you could say that we fit the mold of the classic immigrant family of that era: big and poor, but happy.

My parents both came from the Sicilian village of Monreale, near Palermo. Their families have long histories in the Palermo region, and in 1952 while I was touring Italy I stopped off at the Hall of Records to do a little digging into my roots. I discovered that my great-grandfather on my father's side had been married to a lady named Magdalena Sinatra. Frank Sinatra's father's family came from a Sicilian village not too far away, and it's possible that Sinatra's great-grandfather was my great-grandmother's brother, making him a fourth cousin of mine. After I got back to the States, I told Sinatra this convoluted story when I ran across him at a party. Later in the evening, while we sat across from each other at either end of a long dinner table, he interrupted his conversation several times to look my way, gesture, and shout *"Cousino! Cousino!"*

My mother, Anna Salerno (born Cresenzia Concetta Salerno), was only eight years old when her father left Monreale to try and make a better life for his wife and six children in America. He worked the railroads, dug ditches, and eventually settled in Chicago and became a butcher. It seemed he was always broke no matter how hard he worked, and four years later he had to borrow the money he needed to relieve his loneliness and send for his family. They left Monreale on December 5, 1906, and sailed over third class. They settled into the second floor of a small house on Townsend Street and rented out the bottom rooms to borders to help make ends meet. That was how my mother and father first met.

Pa, John LoVecchio (born Giovanni), had also come over from Sicily in steerage around 1906. He got a job as a water boy for the Chicago Railroad, was eventually promoted to laying rails, and ended up rooming at Townsend Street. He flipped for my mom the moment he saw her, but at first all they could do about it was stare at each other from either end of a little porch in a back alley.

My mother's father was a very strict Italian from the old school, and he'd already promised her hand in marriage to someone else. There had been an engagement party and she was committed. When my father had to leave town to work for the Pennsylvania Railroad for a while, my mother realized how deeply she missed him, and when he returned she went to her father and demanded that her engagement be called off. He was furious. When he found out who she had been moping over he launched into a big speech about how he had known my father's family in Monreale, and that they were low class people unfit to associate with any daughter of his. I don't know if it was the power of true love or plain old-fashioned persistence, but my parents eventually rode out the storm and were married. In the meantime Pa decided that railroad work was a mite too grueling, so he went to trade school and learned to become a barber.

I was born in the house on Townsend Street, but the family soon moved to 1440 North Park, across the street from the Church of the Immaculate Conception and its parochial school. When I was eight, we moved just around the corner to 331 West Schiller and my family stayed there for the next twenty-five years. It was a very ethnic neigh- borhood, and Immaculate Conception certainly catered to a diverse parish in those days.

We had Germanic people living across the street, Italians on one side, French on another, some Swedes around the corner and a few black families living across the street kitty-corner. I don't remember the ethnic jumble ever causing any serious problems. One of my closest friends was a black playmate named Drew. I spent as much time over at his house as he did at mine. There was a strong sense of community and an unspoken feeling that we were all in this together and had to make out as best we could. It was a very happy neighborhood.

Ma was a partner in my grandfather's grocery, although I have no idea where she found the time to work so hard. It seemed to me she was perpetually pregnant.

The kids came thick and fast, and as soon as a newborn arrived the oldest child was rotated half a block down the street to live with our grandparents behind the grocery. My brothers Sam, Frank, Joe, and I all slept together over there in a couple of rollaways, separated from our grandparents by an iron wire with a sheet draped over it (and kids today feel cheated if they don't have their own private telephone!). There was a goat kept out back, as well as a horse for riding to market.

My little brother John came along later and proved to be a handful right from the start. When he was just a few weeks old, I was taking him for a visit with his grandmother when I stumbled coming down the steps and he popped out of his blanket and landed buck naked, but smiling, in a nearby snowdrift. Maybe this was an omen of things to come. When the boys grew older, one of our favorite pastimes was sneaking rides by hopping onto the rear bumpers of passing cars. John tried this once, but missed and was too scared to let go. He was dragged on his kneecaps for nearly six blocks. A little while later, none the wiser, he fell between the slats of a wooden fence he was climbing and nearly forfeited his ability to carry on the LoVecchio name!

When we got a little out of hand, Grandpa Salerno acted as the disciplinarian. He had a terrible temper and was in great shape for a man of his age (he once chased me through the streets for well over a mile because of some infraction I've long since forgotten). When the boom was about to be lowered at home, we often hid by scrambling under his large bed. Grandpa was onto that dodge, however, and used to stick a big broom down there and sweep it back and forth to drive us out. We really weren't the kind of children who needed punishment often, though, and both my grandparent's home and my parent's house were happy places to be, filled with love and the mouth-watering smells of good Sicilian cooking.

I was raised a city boy, but my mom's father had a farm in Benton Harbor, Michigan, and for two summers (when I was five and six) I was exposed to a different way of life. Those were wonderful times. I'd awaken to the smell of fresh bread baking in red brick ovens out in the yard. My Uncle John would squirt milk from a cow's teat straight into my mouth, and my Aunt Jeanette used to make me feel like a big shot by letting me handle the reins on their two-horse buggy. At night there was a symphony of crickets under the clearest sky I'd ever seen. Eventually my mother's brothers felt the lure of the big city and when they all left the farm was sold, bringing my vacations in the country to an end.

Back in Chicago I used to play stickball in the street and baseball in Lincoln Park (we were all Chicago White Sox fans except for my brother John, who was obstinately loyal to the Cubs). In between the running around and playing I suppose I sang to myself too, but no more so than the average child. My family wasn't very musically inclined, although my mother did love the opera and Pa used to take us to Ravinia Park in the summer to hear outdoor performances. On Sundays they would bring me along, and once I even heard the great Caruso himself. Chicago was a good town to grow up in, with the exception of an unfortunate element that plagued the entire community.

Organized crime, "the mob," or whatever you want to call it was a fact of life in the Chicago of the 1920s. Some guys became gangsters through greed, some through necessity. It's not that I was confronted with daily violence, and I certainly didn't read the papers in those days, but there was enough talk and gossip making the rounds for me to be aware that dark, dangerous things were going on. My Uncle Ted used to mysteriously drop out of sight for long stretches at a time, and it was rumored that he was somehow involved.

For a while, my father was Al Capone's personal barber. Capone was the only customer who never visited Pa's shop. When he wanted a shave or a haircut, he would send word and Pa would pack his things into a little bag and be escorted to Capone's place by a couple of henchmen. I suppose no mob boss wants to be surprised by unfriendly visitors while leaning back in a chair with a hot towel around his face. My mother's father, Salvatore Salerno, received some of those unsocial visitors at home one day in an incident that still burns in my memory over sixty years later.

Grandfather Salerno, as I was later to discover through conversations with my mother, occasionally served as something of a peacemaker amongst the warring factions in Chicago. Somebody decided they didn't appreciate his intervention and wanted him out of the way. I was upstairs after school with my grandmother one afternoon when we heard five "BOOMS!" coming in rapid succession from the grocery store below where they lived.

My grandmother, who was in her late fifties at the time, shot down the stairs like a rocket and though I was just a wiry twelve year old I didn't stand a chance of keeping up with her. When I reached the bottom of the stairs I found her cradling Grandpa Salerno's head in her arms. He was stretched out on the sawdust floor, there was blood everywhere, and though I was confused and bewildered I knew immediately that I was staring at death. Grandma screamed at me and my brother Sam (who was only eight) to run for help. We tried, but there was really nothing to be done except clean up. The police later found two pistols that had been tossed under a Nash Coupé parked in front of the grocery. They never arrested the gunmen who did it, but this was because they had been, as Ma phrased it in the parlance of the times, "taken care of" by some rival gangsters.

* * * * * *

Several years before that family tragedy I'd started elementary school at Immaculate Conception, and my first real introduction to music came from a wonderful second grade teacher there named Sister Norbert. She could be a demon and a tyrant at times, but looking back I realize that she was responsible for dinning a lot of fundamental musical concepts into my head. When the fourth grade rolled around, the Monsignor visited our class to recruit new altar boys and voices for the all-boy choir to replace the several members who had recently been lost through graduation. I'd like to be able to say that I volunteered or won a place with a brilliant audition, but the truth is that I was drafted, and grudgingly at that. I quickly grew to love and take pride in my new duties, however, and enjoyed just about every aspect of the job (except for getting up to serve 5:30 Mass!).

I think my first hymn was *Stabat Mater*. I soon learned many more along with *Adeste Fidelis* and other Christmas songs. I was never blessed with that clear, bell-like soprano that choir boys are supposed to have, so I was never given a solo. There was an Irish kid named Eddie Ryan who used to stand next to me and sing with the voice of an angel. He's the one who got all the solos. I remember glancing over at him in mid-song and watching with jealousy as the veins in his neck swelled out on the high notes. Those five years spent in choir were my first major exposure to music, and the experience was a total pleasure. Socializing with the other fellows outside of the church, however, could have its drawbacks.

Every summer the altar boys had a picnic at a seminary in Mt. Carmel, Illinois. There were grounds and fields to play in, a swimming pool, outdoor cooking and things like that. I was standing by the edge of the pool, talking, when in the midst of all the laughing and carrying on somebody

11

My parents at their wedding, 1910.

My maternal grandfather, Salvatore Salerno, who was as-
sasinated by gangsters.

Earliest known photo of Frankie Laine, age six (1919).

Frankie Laine at choir practice. He is in the back row, center,
on the left side of the door frame.

elbowed me into the water. I was twelve years old and thoroughly unacquainted with the fine art of swimming. I fell in at the eight foot mark and though I had the presence of mind to spin in the air and try to catch the edge of the pool, I didn't have the luck to pull it off. When I opened my mouth to yell for help it was already well below the surface. I swallowed a lot of water.

One of the counselors in charge of the group saw me in the pool, but he wanted to make sure that I wasn't just fooling around before he exerted any effort. He stood and watched me come up flailing and gasping for air three times before he casually reached down to grab my wrist and pluck me out. Fortunately, I didn't need any resuscitation. I just wanted to be left alone as I threw up water and tried to pull myself together. I felt nauseous and dizzy for a while, but not too dizzy to realize that I'd better learn how to keep myself afloat. I soon picked up this necessary "survival" skill and learned what marvelous exercise swimming can be, although it was a long, long time before I had regular access to a pool.

* * * * * *

It was around the time we moved to West Schiller Street that I first began to take an active interest in music, wanting to listen to it and seeking out things to hear. I was ten years old and hadn't yet started choir.

The new house came partially furnished, and one of the items included was an old-fashioned wind-up Victrola built into a double cabinet. There was also a stack of old records, and Ma started playing music around the house (there was no radio for us in those days, much less "singing idols of the airwaves" to discover). It was mostly classical stuff, operatic arias by Caruso and the great divas of the time like Galli-Curci, Rosa Ponselle, and Alma Gluck. There were also a few pop Italian records by a fellow named Carlo Buti who had a warm, mellow baritone that was very easy on the ears. He later came to be known as the Bing Crosby of Italy. I enjoyed listening to him, but not nearly as much as I liked one particular record that influenced me profoundly.

I have no idea how the disc made its way into this collection of "high class" music, but thank goodness it did. I can still close my eyes and visualize its blue and purple label. It was a Bessie Smith recording of *Bleeding Hearted Blues*, with *Midnight Blues* on the other side. The first time I laid the needle down on that record I felt cold chills and an indescribable excitement. It was my first exposure to jazz and the blues, although I had no idea at the time what to call those magical sounds. I just knew I had to hear more of them!

I was a pretty conscientious student as a rule, but one day a few years later I skipped class to go downtown to the movies and see Al Jolson in *The Singing Fool*. It was my introduction to that master entertainer, who was then at the peak of his popularity, and he electrified me. After watching him sink to his knees and sing *Sonny Boy*, I knew what I wanted to do with my life. I wanted to be like Jolson and captivate an audience with the power of a song. I was so impressed that I sat through the movie twice until I knew the lyrics and the melody cold. I came home right at the time I usually did after school, and everything was fine until I rounded up my kid brothers into the bedroom for an impromptu performance. I was emoting in my best Jolson manner when Ma appeared in the doorway and demanded to know where I'd learned that tune, figuring correctly that I hadn't picked it up at choir practice. The truth came out, resulting in one of the only times that I can remember her getting mad enough to smack me. I remained a loyal Jolson fan, though, and would have loved to hear more if there had been any money to buy records.

Back in the schoolroom my grades began to drop, but this wasn't due to musical distractions. One of the Sisters had an interesting ranking system for her classes. She sat the best student in the first seat of the first row and the worst in the last seat of the last row. The rest of us were spread out in between depending on how well we were doing. When I was near the blackboard everything was great, but I was lost if my ranking put me in one of the back rows. My Uncle John took me to the optometrist and it turned out that I was extremely nearsighted. Glasses let me see that I had been missing a lot and, except when performing, I have worn them ever since.

After elementary school I went on to Lane Technical High School where I went out for track and basketball. I didn't have much speed, but I could really last and started to develop into a pretty fair long distance runner. Looking back, I think this brief fling with running was when I started to develop the lung power and breath control that helped me so much as a singer. As dearly as I loved them, I had to give up both track and basketball after about five months when the always tight money situation at home became even more desperate than usual. Pa found me an after school job at a drug store run by John Caravelli, one of his barbering customers. I worked three hours every night, all day Saturday, and three hours every other Sunday morning for the princely wage of three bucks a week. School and work became the sum total of my existence until I was about fifteen years old.

My time in the choir and my introductions to Bessie Smith and Al Jolson really fueled my interest in music. I found I had a tremendous instinctive empathy for jazz music and, as much as I admired Jolson the performer, I never really wanted to sing in his style. I wanted to be more like the icing on my musical cake, a gentleman who had just hit town from New Orleans. This was in 1928, and from records and the radio I heard a song called *West End Blues*. The singing and playing of Louis Armstrong sent me through the roof! I later recorded *West End Blues* on the first album I ever made, and back in Chicago in the late '20s I started singing jazz tunes to anyone who'd listen.

I mainly sang to entertain at gatherings of my family, but one day a friend of mine named Tom Henahan invited me over to his house for his sister Teresa's 18th birthday party. At 16 he was a year older than I was, as were most of the people at the party, but through Tom and his sister I was accepted as one of the crowd. A fellow named Tony Benson had brought a tipple to the party, and a group of about thirty people gathered in the living room to sing songs (the tipple was a "bastard" instrument that's seldom seen today. It was small, eight-stringed, and sounded like a combination of a tenor guitar and a ukelele). We launched into an Italian-flavored pop song of the day called *Mia Bella Rosa*, and gradually the other voices in the room dropped out until only mine was left. It was the first time I had sung solo to an audience that didn't consist of my relatives, but I was too caught up in the emotion of that pretty little song to notice. I started to cry, and the tears were rolling down my cheeks when I finished singing to an audience that had grown deathly still.

Every girl in the place started bawling, and every guy seemed stunned at what they had heard, as if this was the last thing they expected from the kid. After a long silence, everyone began talking at once. "Hey Frank," they shouted, "Sing it again! Sing another one!" I sang it again, then ran through nearly every other song I knew and after that I was really in solid with this crowd. Every time there was a party or a picnic in the making, I was included in the plans because I could entertain. They were a fun group to hang around with, and their favorite stomping ground played an important part in my life.

The Merry Garden Ballroom was on Chicago's North Side. It cost me fourteen cents to get there and back, and when Ma only had seven cents I used to steal a ride on the "El." The Garden was the place where everyone rendez-

17

voused to dance and have a good time. They had a great house band, the Joe Kayser Orchestra, and it still boggles my mind to recall the musicians who made up that group: Dave Rose was on piano, Gene Krupa on drums, Frankie Trumbauer on C melody sax, Frank Teschemacher, the Benny Goodman of his day, on clarinet (I later studied with him for a year and a half), Muggsy Spanier on trumpet, and a fellow named Johnny Maitland on bass. They also had a regular vocalist, Frank Sylvano, with a bouncy style that really knocked me out.

My friends used to clamor for me to get up and sing with the band, and occasionally they'd give in and let me do a song or two. My first time on stage at the ballroom was with the visiting Charlie Agnew Orchestra. I was so nervous that my voice cracked like a dry twig on a high note during *Old New England Moon*. I was red faced with embarrassment and thought I would die, but the over-enthusiastic applause of my friends after I was finished helped soothe my jangled nerves considerably.

On holidays and other special occasions guest bands would come in and alternate with the house band. I saw the Paul Whiteman Orchestra there and had my breath taken away when Mildred Bailey sang *Rockin' Chair*. She became a great favorite of mine, and for a long time after that *Rockin' Chair* was *my* song. Very few people have ever been able to read a song lyric the way that lady did. I also saw Cab Calloway when he passed through on Lincoln's Birthday to front what I now know was a pick-up band of local musicians (at the time I just assumed they were his regular men). What an incredibly dynamic performer! I was really thrilled with the way he wailed and strutted around the bandstand while singing *Ploddin' Along*. His showmanship had a lasting impact on me.

Our crowd used to hang out at the Merry Garden five nights a week. We took dance courses and became so proficient at the latest steps that Jack Lund and Ethel

Kendall, the owners, hired some of us to teach dancing on Tuesday nights. In exchange for this service we received passes that allowed us to come in for free and stay as long as we liked any day of the week. So in 1928 I became a sort of half-assed dance instructor. By the following year that free admission was really coming in handy, because "free" was just about all that anyone could afford.

The stock market crash of 1929 and the Great Depression which followed hit Chicago very hard. Things were getting worse at home and I had to get another job to bring in more money. Once again I found work through a friend of Pa's, this time at the International Harvester Company. They started me out in the mail room for fifteen bucks a week, then after six months they raised my salary by two and a half bucks and made me a bookkeeper.

Math wasn't exactly my strong suit. If I had been put to work counting money I probably would have garbled their books beyond salvation. Instead, I found myself counting plows and tractors and figuring out how many were going out on different ships. The economic situation was getting bleaker all the time, however, and after another six months they had to let me go.

I was unemployed, broke, and at a loss over what to try next when I caught a glimpse of a strange light at the end of the tunnel: A marathon dance came to Chicago.

TWO

MARATHON DAYS

The marathon dance craze that swept the country in the early '30s is a bit difficult to explain to those who didn't live through it. Many people today have a bad impression of the marathons from a pretty grim picture made in the late 1960s called *They Shoot Horses, Don't They?* My experiences in these events were different and much happier than those depicted in the movie. You must remember that for people who had the stamina the dances were a handy way to pick up a buck during some very tough times.

There were two ways to make money at a marathon dance contest. The most common, of course, was to enter as a contestant and keep dancing for all you were worth in the hope that you and your partner would be among the last few couples on the floor and earn a share of the prize money. The other way was to entertain the folks who had come to watch the dancers compete. Many entertainers besides yours truly got their start in the marathons — singing, tap dancing, and performing comedy skits for the money that would be tossed to them from the bleachers.

My first glimpse inside this crazy world left me feeling put out. The marathons came to Chicago around 1930, and one afternoon my little social group and I gathered at the Merry Garden Ballroom only to find out that we were being banished to the annex. We were told to go do our thing in there because of some big happening in the main ballroom that the management didn't want disrupted. Needless to say, this didn't go down too well with any of us. The Merry Garden had been our hangout for years! Griping got us nowhere, however, so we settled down in our new environment and made the best of it. Once, out of curiosity, I poked my head into the main ballroom and saw makeshift seating for about 5,000 people, most of it filled. There was a large clear area in the middle of the floor for the dancers, who shuffled about in pairs with printed number cards on their backs. Eddie Gilmartin, the manager of the ballroom, was standing on a raised platform with a microphone in his hand and seemed to be acting as a master of ceremonies. It was an interesting spectacle, but not intriguing enough to draw me away from my buddies in the annex.

Then one Saturday night there was a "Night Of Stars" type event for a charitable organization in downtown Chicago. Nearly every performer in the city attended, and that included the small-time acts who did their stuff for the marathon audiences. The contestants were frequently entertainers themselves, but at this point in the dance things had narrowed down to just three couples with no real talent except endurance amongst them.

The management at the ballroom was caught shorthanded, and they were frantically searching for people who could do something to keep their audiences from fidgeting. Somebody reminded Mr. Gilmartin (or just plain "Gil" as I always used to call him) that there was a kid named LoVecchio giving dance lessons in the annex who could sing a little bit. Gil rushed over and pulled me out, and before I had time to take it all in I found myself on a bandstand in front of 10,000 skeptical eyes that didn't look too excited to see me.

There was a quartet on the stand led by a trumpet player named Vic Abbs, who later became a good friend of mine. He had with him a drummer named Leroy Buck, pianist Jess Stacy, who went on to great success with the Benny Goodman Orchestra, and a bassist whose name I've never been able to recall. I was one nervous seventeen year old as I walked over to Jess, who smiled at me reassuringly and asked "What would you like to sing, kid?"

There was a song that was popular at the time called *Beside An Open Fireplace*. It had been written by Will Osborne, a very good songwriter and a popular singing orchestra leader who never quite got out from under the shadow of his rival in that era, Rudy Vallee. I loved the tune and suggested that we try it. "What key?" asked Jess. Now, it should tell you a lot about my expertise at this point that I had no idea what the hell he was talking about. Key? What did he mean by "key?" I sheepishly confessed that I really didn't know, but Jess put me at ease. Many good musicians can get an idea of the way someone sings from the way they sound when they talk, and Jess said, "Well, you sound about average. Let's try it in E flat, the original key."

By this time the crowd was restless, having no idea who this "unannounced attraction" was or what he intended to do for them. We launched into the song and after four bars I could sense instinctively that I had their undivided attention. *Fireplace* was a sentimental tune, and the lyrics choked me up just like they had when I sang *Mia Bella Rosa* at Teresa Henahan's birthday party. When I finished the tears were rolling down my cheeks and the place was quiet as a tomb. For a little while nothing, and I mean *nothing*, happened. There was no reaction of any kind from the audience, much less applause, and my tears of emotion

23

turned to tears of shame. At this age I didn't know anything about show business phrases like "I bombed" or "I died." All I could do was stand there speechless and think to myself, "Oh my God, all these people really didn't like me."

I'd taken off my glasses before I started singing, so I was half-blind to begin with. My crying, mingled with a numbing depression, left me feeling lost in a haze and all I wanted to do was get out of it and go quietly bury myself somewhere. I managed to mumble a thank you to Jess before I started to grope my way towards the exit. I had just reached the dance floor when the crowd broke loose.

There was absolute pandemonium in the Merry Garden Ballroom. Yelling, cheering, and foot stomping like I had never heard before. Pretty soon Gilmartin made his way through the crowd and threw his arms around me in a hug. He stepped back and I saw that I wasn't the only one in the place with tears in his eyes. "Jesus Christ, kid, that was fantastic! Go back and sing another one!" he urged. I was too bewildered to make any sense of it all, and was still asking him if he meant it when he pushed me back on stage. Jess Stacy was beaming at me. "My, that was great, kid. What do you want to do now?" I felt ten feet off the ground as the band struck up *Coquette*, my first of five encores that night.

The whole experience was a magical one. That evening was one of those rare occasions that you can look back on and clearly recognize as a turning point in your life.

After my "debut," things changed for me at the Merry Garden. I was hired by the marathon, but not as a singer. Instead, I filled an immediate opening they had for a "trainer." A marathon trainer basically shepherded sleeping contestants to and from their segregated cots (men on one side of the room, women on the other) and also ran little errands for them. Despite the precautions, a lot of women wanted company in the early morning when things were slow and no one was paying much attention. You might say that it was during these wee hours at the marathons that I attended my finishing school in the facts of life.

The management wanted me to sing, too, and I had plenty of opportunities every night. Between 8:00 pm and midnight the contestants themselves put on shows and after that the "free-lancers" like myself got a chance. This was in November of 1930. I was learning songs like *Body and Soul* and *Stardust*, mostly tunes that were to go on to become great jazz standards.

As the contest began winding down, Gilmartin approached me with an interesting proposition. When this marathon was over he was planning to go to Baltimore to start a new one and he asked me to come along as a contestant. I would get to sing, and he also promised to teach me how to handle the M.C. duties. If I couldn't last as a contestant (and I could tell that he was sure I'd fold), there would always be a job waiting for me as a trainer and things would be just like they'd been in Chicago. This seemed to be a great opportunity. I'd not only be working on the fringes of show business, I'd be working period, which was more than a lot of people could boast of at the time.

In 1931 we were in the depths of the Depression and things were tough at home. I'd lost my job as a bookkeeper for International Harvester. While struggling to support a family of nine on $21 a week my father lost his barbershop. We eventually went on relief, but that only lasted for a week. It made my mother desperate with shame and she spent the entire time crying. Finally, Pa proclaimed, "To hell with it, we'll starve first!" With things this bad I figured that one less mouth to feed wouldn't hurt the family a bit, and if I managed to scrape some money together I could send it back to Chicago to make things easier.

I also knew for certain by now that I wanted to be a singer. Pa didn't consider this to be a very practical ambition and wanted me to become a pharmacist or an architect. He was strictly from the "get-a-job-and-save-five-bucks-a-week" school of thought. Ma, God love her, knew how much my dreams meant to me, and just how badly I wanted them to come true. She supported me all the way. To help smooth things over, Gil spent a pleasant April afternoon at my house spinning tales of glowing rewards and assuring my parents that I would be well taken care of. Soon, at the tender age of 18, I was off on the road to Baltimore.

* * * * * *

The dance marathons were held in all kinds of different circumstances (I was in a ridiculous one at Stamford, Connecticut, that took place in an undersized Elk's lodge hall). The Baltimore marathon was held at a sports facility, and before it was over everyone who participated picked up a nasty foot infection that caused the contestants to drop out like flies. To make matters worse for me, on my first day in town I managed to come down with a bad case of poison ivy while sightseeing! My assigned partner, a girl named Ruth Donnelly, only lasted six days. This left me as a solo contestant for the next ninety days, shuffling around all by my lonesome, scratchy self while waiting to inherit another partner. We all stayed on the dance floor for 45 minutes out of every hour, getting fifteen minutes off to go to the bathroom, eat, or maybe lie back on a table while someone rubbed cold cream on our feet. Contestants burned up so much energy that we were fed eight times a day, four heavy meals and four snacks. During the shows, the dancers that weren't performing sneaked off to grab a little sleep. Then they'd come back and quite literally dance the night away.

You learned to survive by making adjustments quickly. It wasn't long before I got the hang of sleeping while standing on my feet and dancing. It wasn't as difficult as it sounds, particularly if your partner could help you out. My favorite marathon partner was a girl named Florence Shannon who only weighed 98 pounds. When she went to sleep I could just put a finger behind her back and walk her around the floor with me. On the other hand, some partners were "lugs" and could be a real curse. Lugs felt like a sack of lead when they went to sleep, and you had to lock your hands behind their back and drag them around for long periods at a time. My shoulders are slightly rounded even now thanks to several lugs from my marathon days.

At the Baltimore marathon, things eventually reached the point where there were just a few couples and 22 guys left soloing like me. The promoters wanted to thin out the pack so they ran a "grind," meaning that we were all kept shuffling constantly without any breaks for any reason until only the finalists were left. It finally narrowed down to just three couples and me. When a fellow named George Jacobs dropped out I was assigned his wife Betty as a partner, and we went on to win the damned thing after a total of 106 days. My staying power surprised me a little bit, and it flat out shocked Gilmartin. Here was a full-fledged marathon dancer who could entertain, too! Gil thought he'd found a gold mine and was anxious to hustle his discovery into other contests.

I thought I'd stumbled across a gold mine myself when I was handed $2800 as my share of the prize money. This small fortune made for quite a homecoming. My parents could hardly believe it when after all those months I came back and laid that kind of coin on the table. The LoVecchios had themselves a well deserved, New Orleans-style Mardi Gras on Chicago's North Side.

The next marathon I took part in was a flop because there weren't enough citizens in the town of Willow Grove, Pennsylvania, who were willing to shell out one

Age 18, My first "professional photograph," taken for publicity at the Baltimore Marathon. I thought the cigarette made me look grown up.

With the ever-so-light Florence Shannon.

1932: Shaking hands with the vanquished Joie Ray while his partner Mary Fenton (left) does the same with mine, Ruth Smith.

Horseback riding with partner Ruth Smith after we set the
world's record for Marathon Dancing at Young's Million Dollar Pier in Atlantic City, 1932.

thin dime to see what was billed as "a thrilling display of local endurance." From there we went on to North Bergen, New Jersey, where I got so sick that by the second day of the marathon I was running a fever of 105. I wanted to tough it out, but the fever wouldn't cooperate. I went to take a quick nap and had my friends promise to wake me up. They felt sorry for me and decided to let me rest, and as a result I slept for nearly twenty-four hours and was disqualified. It's just as well that things worked out that way. If I had tried to hang in there and survived, the promoters would have kicked me off the floor anyway because of the health threat I posed to the other dancers.

When you were part of a troop like I was, and you had to drop out of a marathon early, there was a headquarters in Atlantic City where you could go and be taken care of for a few months between contests. I stayed at a place called Mom Smith's Boarding House and was given a little spending money to help tide me over. I spent my days wandering around the boardwalk, which coincidentally became the site of my next and most memorable marathon ever.

On May 27, 1932, we started a new contest at Young's Million Dollar Pier. I was assigned a partner I had never met, a girl named Ruthie Smith. We not only won but went on to set a world's record together. We danced until October 19, a grand total of 3,501 hours. That's 145 days! This feat was duly noted for years in the *Guiness Book Of World Records*. Let me tell you, it was not an easy record to set.

My main competition in Atlantic City was a man named Joie (pronounced "Joey") Ray, a former Olympic miler who was a very well known and popular figure at the time. Age was on my side, however, because he was 38 and I was only 19. An opening field of 101 teams eventually came down to just Ray and me and our partners. When none of us showed any signs of weakening, the promoter of the event started getting worried. He was a fellow named George L. Ruty, and he had only hired the hall for one more day. It was decided to bring things to a head by running a grind.

Before the grind started Ruthie and I ate a good meal but didn't have anything to drink. Joie Ray did, and that was his fatal mistake. As the grind extended, so did Ray's bladder. Inevitably nature took its course and, since the man wasn't allowed to leave the floor, he wet his pants and was disqualified. Ruthie and I became the world champions and split a very handsome prize. I've never seen her in all the years since, though I've heard that she's living in Fort Lauderdale, Florida, today.

After this triumph, I was really top dog among my fellow singers and comedians who followed the marathon circuit. Our next stop was New Haven, Connecticut, where I was paired with a fantastic dancer named Ruth Johnstone. She and I put on dancing exhibitions featuring the Lindy Hop and other current dance fads. All those nights spent kicking up my heels at the Merry Garden Ballroom really came in handy. There was a tremendous Italian population in New Haven which went out of its way to make me feel comfortable and at home. I made plenty of new friends and had a marvelous time. It was also while in New Haven that I first came across a little girl singing on the radio by the name of Baby Rose Marie. She grew up to become the Rose Marie we remember from *The Dick Van Dyke Show* and *Hollywood Squares*, but at that time she was only nine years old and could sing the hell out of ballads like *Willow Weep For Me*.

I couldn't believe that a young kid could sing with such great jazz feeling. I was so impressed with her rendition of *Willow* that I started doing it at the marathons. A lot of the singers at the marathons had theme songs which they were identified with. In New Haven and at the next contest in Lakewood, Pennsylvania, I was singing mainly Bing

31

Crosby tunes like *I Surrender Dear* and *Straight From the Shoulder, Right From the Heart.* At the time crooning was a brand new thing and I was just knocked out by Bing's sound. I used to imitate him so closely that people said I sounded more like Crosby than Crosby did. When Louis Armstrong came out with *Sleepy Time Down South*, I included that in my repertoire at Atlantic City and fell even deeper under the spell of that genius' style and phrasing. Later, after the dance marathons had turned into walkathons, I began featuring *Wagon Wheels*. I would belt out this Western ditty at the drop of a Stetson. My landlady in Pottsville, Pennsylvania, an otherwise motherly soul named Mrs. Mary Lurwick, became so fed up that she started shouting back her hope that the wagon wheels would soon turn around and run me over.

All together I participated in a total of 14 marathons, three of which were flops. In the others I came in first three times, second once, fifth twice, and ended up being knocked out of the running for one infraction or another in the rest. A successful marathon contestant could often pick up a sponsor, and there were also opportunities to sell photographs of yourself and your partner on the back of picture postcards for a nice profit. As bizarre as the whole business sounds today, it was a decent method of keeping body and soul together during the Depression. I made firm and lasting friendships during this period, and came away from it all with many fond memories of characters like Frank Miller, a 67 year old extrovert who could outdance any young girl paired with him. He always took whatever money he won straight to the horse races, where he usually left it.

I especially remember the night of November 5, 1934, when I was asked to be the emcee of the dance-a-thon unit I was with. This was a great break and I gave it my best shot, but I was too inexperienced at that sort of thing and felt awkward. They fired me and hired a skinny young kid to take my place. This guy was pretty green himself, but he was very funny. He performed a hilarious pantomime about dunking doughnuts that absolutely fractured audiences. His name was Red Skelton.

In the beginning the marathons were fairly innocent affairs, but after a while they began to evolve into something a little more brutal. In 1933 at Bridgeport, Connecticut, the contest turned into a walkathon, and then sprints were added. I stopped wearing socks to help stave off foot infections. These walkathons were eventually transformed by a man named Leo Seltzer into the Roller Derby games that enjoyed such popularity on television years ago. In fact, after my last marathon with George L. Ruty and company in Elizabeth, New Jersey, I went home to Chicago to find that Seltzer was putting on a contest there at the Arcadia Ballroom. This was his last marathon before he switched over to the roller derby and, although I loved to skate, I didn't want any part of this new trend.

At the Arcadia, in my last go around as a marathon contestant, I managed to hurt my ankle pretty badly and ended up spending the entire eight weeks that I was in the contest wrapped up with bandages and tape. My mother was frightened by the exhaustion she saw in my eyes, so in 1935 I quit the marathons for good.

Before I left I became acquainted with a precocious little girl in the contest who was already developing into a mature vocalist at the age of 14. She would follow me around like a little puppy after every song I sang and pepper me with questions: "Why did you pick that tune? Why did you phrase like that? How come. . . how come. . . how come?" Of course, when they found out that she was underage they pulled her right off the floor, but her brief stint in the contest marked the beginning of my association with a lady who became one of our great jazz stylists, Anita O'Day.

The Marathons may never have landed my name in *Variety,* but I got a lot out of them. I gained experience, insights into human nature, and learned how to handle big crowds (Young's Million Dollar Pier had a seating capacity of 12,000). Some of the attention I received back in those days helped light a spark of hope that maybe I had a shot at bigger and better things.

When I reflect on it, dancing has been almost as good to me over the years as singing. After all, 15 years down the road I exchanged some very special words with a very special lady while dancing to the strains of *Blue Moon* at the Cocoanut Grove. I'll tell you more about that later. At this stage I was still a hell of a long way from the Cocoanut Grove.

By 1935 I had been paying my dues for five years and was certain that success, like prosperity, was "just around the corner." I had no idea that well over a decade of scuffling lay ahead of me.

THREE

HARD TIMES AND FALSE STARTS

Soon after dropping out of the marathon at the Arcadia, I traveled across town to check out the Ball of Fire, a little nightclub that used to sit at 63rd and Broadway in Chicago. Anita O' Day had managed to get a job singing there, and she was working with several performers who had also worked the marathons. Dick Buckley, a nutty comic who dubbed himself "Lord Buckley" (and later became a cult figure of the counterculture), used to emcee the shows. They also had a wild guitar player named Jim Jam (who in addition strummed a mean banjo while performing eccentric dances). They tried to get me a job there too, but the club's payroll couldn't handle four entertainers.

After the evening show we would spend the rest of the night hopping around town and visiting other clubs, where I often got a chance to get up and do a song or two. A lot of people heard me and I started getting some good word of mouth publicity. Besides, Anita and her friends were a wild bunch and a lot of fun to hang around with.

The only time I've ever been stoned in my life was off of the marijuana fumes I inhaled secondhand when Anita and Dick broke out a couple of joints one night in the back of a cramped taxi on the way to a club. I remember feeling giddy and lightheaded when we arrived, and I know for a fact that Anita was feeling no pain. As we pulled up to the curb she said, "I want to check things out, Frank. Hold this beer for me, will ya?" and then she tossed her purse into my lap.

Our nightclubbing came to an end when out of the blue I got a wire from a trombone player in Stamford, Connecticut, whom I had become friendly with while working in the marathon there. He said that he was starting a band to fill a ballroom opening in Coscob, Connecticut, and wanted to know if I was free to work with him. I'd enjoyed good regional popularity there during the marathon, so I took the bus fare he sent and headed East. Unfortunately, we just didn't draw. In February of 1936 things were still tough. Nobody seemed interested in the band, and the people who came to see me again only came once. After a week we folded, and a fan who liked our music helped me get a job to tide me over in the plant where he worked, the Zapon Synthetic Leather Company, a small subsidiary of Dupont.

Frankly, a synthetic leather factory does not provide the most aromatic working environment in the world. The work was not only smelly, it was hard. In seven days spent wrapping rolls of synthetic leather for shipment, I went from 194 to 166 pounds. I couldn't have stayed there if not for some additional shipping clerk duties which provided a desperately needed rest from the drudgery. I spent my days at the plant and at night I frequented a little German club where a fiddle player named Pete Viggiano (who in better days had conducted Stamford's symphony orchestra) led a trio that played music on Wednesdays, Saturdays, and Sundays. I sat in and sang with them, and it proved a fascinating and important experience for me.

German music can be very lively, and the management wanted everything the band played to really move. Pete's instructions were to alternate between German and American tunes, and even the American ballads had to be played kind of up-tempo for dancing. A lot of people requested ballads, and since they had to be played faster, I had to sing them faster. Suddenly, I was doing lilting love songs as out-and-out rhythm tunes. I remember Kate Smith singing *By the River Saint Marie* and emphasizing the slow, gorgeous melody. Well, in Stamford we were swinging through it with an entirely different pulse and beat, sounding much more like it came out when I recorded it for Mercury Records in 1946.

I discovered that I really enjoyed this style of singing, and got a kick out of feeling my way around new songs while learning them at a quick tempo. I'd even find myself telling Pete to "take it up" on occasion. I was inching toward my own individual style, and after thirteen months at the factory I began to get restless. I'd managed to sock away enough of my $25 a week salary to stake a fling at New York City, so I quit my job and headed north.

In those days New York's 52nd Street was known as "Swing Street," and the rage of 52nd Street was a clarinetist from my old Chicago neighborhood named Joe Marsala. He was playing at a club called the Hickory House where they had Sunday afternoon jam sessions. The first thing I did after hitting town was rent myself a little room and head straight for the Hickory House, where I talked them into letting me on stage for a few numbers. I sang *Rosetta, Shine*, and *Stardust*. Red Allen, a great trumpet player, was so impressed that he said, "Gee, Joe, this kid is great. You ought to hire him." Marsala suggested that I try to come down to the club more often and promised that occasionally he would call me on stage to sing. For eight solid weeks I slicked myself up in a tuxedo every night and planted myself on a bar stool at the Hickory

House. Not once, *not once* in all that time was I called on to perform. What can you do when you're built up and then ignored like that? Eventually my money ran out and I had to head home to Chicago.

Before leaving New York, I did manage to land a few jobs teaming up with a piano player named Art Hodes. I met Art at one of the Hickory House jam sessions and we decided to work up an act together. We rehearsed in the basement of an old saloon on 51st Street, and the owner of the joint was so stingy that he charged us a quarter just to turn on the light so we could see our music. An agent booked us into the New Paramount Grill in Passaic, New Jersey. We had to take the subway, the ferry, and then a bus just to get there, and we each only pulled down thirty bucks a week for our trouble.

For reasons that I never understood, the owner of the place assumed that I was Jewish and Art was Italian (when in fact the opposite was true). He was an Italian himself, and one night when someone came in and requested *Return To Sorrento* he realized that I was, too. After that he couldn't do enough for us, and things looked great until one night when business was slow and he challenged me to a game of checkers. Apparently he considered himself to be an all-time champion, and when I creamed him he got so mad that he fired us! There must be a moral in there somewhere, but I can't see it.

Art and I moved on to a burlesque show at a theater called the Crawford House in Boston. We did three ninety-minute shows a night. It was a non-union job, however, and Art didn't want to get in trouble so he had to quit after two weeks. Without him, I had no choice but to head home and regroup.

The first thing I did back in Chicago was look up my old marathon mentor, Eddie Gilmartin. I found out that he was now managing the Trianon Ballroom on the South

Side. The orchestra playing there belonged to Ted Weems and featured that latest singing sensation, a kid who sounded just like Bing Crosby named Perry Como.

Gil introduced me to Ted and Perry so they'd remember my name in case any opportunities came up and sure enough, three weeks later Perry received a very tempting offer to join Paul Whiteman and his Orchestra, the band where Perry's idol Bing Crosby got his start.

Whiteman offered Perry a few hundred bucks a week more than Weems was paying, and every dollar really counted in those days. Perry was happy singing with Ted, so Whiteman put a deadline on his offer to force a decision. Perry arranged for me to audition for Weems as a possible replacement, but he decided to stay on with the band at the last minute when Ted matched Whiteman's offer. This left me out in the cold again, but Perry felt sorry for me and came up with an idea.

He called a bandleader in Cleveland named Freddy Carlone who he'd worked with before he was discovered by Weems. Perry spent $1.25 giving me a big build-up on a long distance phone call and Carlone agreed to give me a chance. Later Perry wouldn't let me reimburse him for the call, and to this day he's never let me pay him back. It's a joke between us now, and every time we run across each other I make the offer and he replies, "You're going to owe me that until the day you die!"

After a big send-off, I arrived in Cleveland with high hopes that were quickly shot down. Carlone turned out to have a Guy Lombardo-style orchestra. That's fine for people who love that kind of music, but I had been developing in a very different direction. When I heard the reed section playing a shade sharp to get that saccharine Lombardo sound, it rasped me like fingernails drawn across a chalkboard. Freddy was equally unnerved by the songs I asked him to play for me. "Frank, we just don't do that kind of music," he protested. I had no choice but to do things his way, and every time I got up to sing a song I wanted to sink through the floorboards. This uncomfortable partnership just wasn't meant to be. We lasted through the holidays, Christmas and New Years, at a place called Freddy's Cafe on Vine Street. Then the manager fired the lot of us.

So I began 1938 unemployed and broke in Cleveland. I went over to the Ace of Clubs, a little spot on Cleveland's East Side, to see a pianist named Murray Arnold (he later played the Sky Roof of the Desert Inn in Las Vegas, but at the time he was only eighteen and being talked up as one of the finest accompanists in the business). There I met a lady who'd been a nurse at the marathon in Atlantic City. She reintroduced herself and when I told her my situation she kindly offered to help. It turned out that she knew the owner of the place, a Mr. Katz, and she convinced him to give me a chance. I had a wonderful time there for exactly one week before a fire burned the Ace of Clubs to the ground.

Before the blaze I'd become friendly with another singer who worked at the club named Zip Howe (with that stage name you'd think she'd be a stripper!). She had a friend named Judy Moreland who was singing at a place called Lindsey's Sky Bar on Euclid Avenue. They had decided to go to New York together and offered to get me an audition at Lindsey's before they left so that I would have first crack at the job that would be opening up. My try out went well, I got the spot, and thus began five months of absolute musical heaven for me.

The piano player at Lindsey's was named Art Cutlip. He and I enjoyed an instantaneous rapport. He loved the way I sang and I thought that he was a fantastic player. On slow nights when there wasn't too much business we would try to stump each other on song titles. When he threw one at me that I didn't know I'd ask, "All right, what key would

I sing it in?" (by now I'd figured out that particular mystery). He'd tell me and then we'd mark it down. Slowly we assembled a book of about one thousand songs, so my repertoire grew to be pretty enormous.

A friend of Louis Armstrong's named Hoyt Kline used to come in and give me more tips on which songs I should learn. I started doing *Shine*, later a gold record for me at Mercury, through the prompting of Hoyt Kline and Art Cutlip. Art taught me *Blue Turning Grey Over You*. We even worked out my own version of *West End Blues*, which I had learned so long ago from Louis Armstrong's record. Kline began to urge me to go on to New York, but I was reluctant. "I've already been," I reminded him, "and I don't like it there. I starved in New York."

After five months of their encouragement, however, my confidence was high and the Big Apple didn't seem so formidable any more. Armed with $40 and a letter of introduction from Hoyt to some "big-time" radio publicity man, I headed off for my second shot at New York. With my club experience and those new songs, I figured I'd be swinging in about a week.

It took me three days to get in to see the radio executive, and fifteen minutes for him to show me the door. After that it wasn't long before I used up my pathetic little bankroll going from club to club for auditions. Things soon got very tough. I would sneak into hotels and sleep on the floor. In fact, I was bodily thrown out of 11 different New York hotels. I stayed in YMCAs and with anyone who would let me flop. Eventually I was down to my last four cents, and my bed became a roughened wooden bench in Central Park. I used my four pennies to buy four tiny Baby Ruth candy bars and rationed myself to one a day.

A New York police detective named Henry Brown took pity on me and brought me into a restaurant to fill up. I did so gratefully, but a bit too enthusiastically. My poor stomach wasn't used to all that food and I had to throw it up. Things had never looked quite this bleak before when a friend suddenly came through with an audition for radio station WINS.

I went in and sang *Shine*, *Rosetta*, and *Marie* with the station's organist, Hank Sylvern. After I'd finished the program director, Jack Coombs, came up and asked me my name. I told him Frank LoVecchio and he shook his head and said that wouldn't do. It was too foreign sounding, and too much of a mouthful for the studio announcers. He decided on "Lane," and I individualized it a little by throwing in an "i" to make it Laine. Frank was stretched out to Frankie to avoid confusion with another singer at the station, a girl named Frances Lane (Dorothy Kirsten, the opera singer, was there too, and Dinah Shore sang at nearby WNEW under the name Fanny Rose). That's how Francesco LoVecchio became Frankie Laine, although I've never had my given name legally changed. I still sign both versions on important documents. I've found over the years that the distinction helps me to keep a good balance between my professional and personal lives.

Jack Coombs offered me three half-hour live broadcasts a week. It was customary to sing for free at these small stations, to perform for the publicity value, but Jack could see that I was in pretty desperate financial straits and worked out a five dollar a week salary for me. This was exactly the amount I needed for a little room in a boarding house across the street from the Plymouth Hotel. Unfortunately, my social security started during this period, and the five cents deducted from my paycheck meant I had to hustle up an extra nickle every week to pay the rent. I'd also fallen into the habit of eating once in a while, and that was another expense to worry about.

One afternoon I was walking down 49th Street with a solitary quarter in my pocket when the aroma from a restaurant named Cosmo's Spaghetti House drew me inside. The owner, Sal Peppe, was on the cash register and he engaged me in conversation (I'm sure it was because I looked hungry and tired). He asked me my name and when I told him he looked pleasantly surprised. "You're Frankie Laine? I just heard you sing *Shine* on WINS. You feel free to come in anytime, eat and sign the tab. You can pay me when you make it big. I *know* you are going to make it big." This was quite a godsend. I ate at Cosmo's and signed the tab for three months. I never had the guts to order anything but the cheapest thing on the menu, which put me on a steady diet of spaghetti and meatballs. Nowadays I'm probably the only Italian around who can't even look at a plate of spaghetti. (Years later, when Sal had moved out to Los Angeles, I tried to repay his kindness by having him cater the "wrap parties" that were thrown after I'd finished my musicals at Columbia).

About this time I ran into Nita Moore, who worked in a music store and used to come in to see me when I was in Cleveland. She was a very dear friend of Jimmy Dorsey's, and Dorsey was in the process of casting around for a new girl singer for his band. I had told Nita that I was New York bound, and she urged me to keep my eyes and ears open. When I first hit town and made the rounds, I'd auditioned at a little club called the Village Barn for a bandleader with the improbable name of Larry Funk.

This was April or May of 1938, and all the girl singers were trying to sound just like Billie Holiday (who had a profound influence on me as well). On the bandstand of the Village Barn I saw the most gorgeous, blonde eighteen year old singer that you could ever hope to find. She was giving out in her best Holiday style, but she didn't have it anywhere near as good as Billie. Still, she knew how to sell a song and with what she had to offer visually she could satisfy any bandleader. I made a mental note and when I ran into Nita again on 49th Street the first thing she asked was, "Did you hear anybody?" I told her what I had found

43

With Billie Holiday outside the the Bop City nightclub in New York, 1949.

and she and Dorsey went down there that night and hired
her on the spot. That was the beginning of big things for
Helen O'Connell. I was left biding my time, and in the
interim WINS decided that they no longer needed a jazz
singer so they let me go.

While making the rounds I'd met and become friends
with Jean Goldkette, a famous bandleader who had seen
better days. He'd been one of the first fellows to have a
string of bands under his name, and he went through
something like twenty-eight different bands touring the
Midwest as the Jean Goldkette Orchestra. He used to
record on Gennett Records, where Bix Beiderbecke made
some of the sides he justly became so famous for. Jean was
full of stories about the various jazz greats who had passed

through his ranks, and he told me some wild tales about Bix and the other giants who I'd listened to for years. In 1929 Jean lost everything in the stock market crash. His band became the Casa Loma Orchestra after he went bankrupt. He liked the way I sang so we signed a personal management deal, which looked like a very big step in the right direction.

Unfortunately for both of us, this was a difficult and demanding period for Jean. He was working with a great composer named Otto Cesana on "Rhapsody in Rhythm," what he hoped would be an important comeback concert for him at Carnegie Hall. He asked me to help out as his librarian. I ended up hauling around a great big trunk of his music all over town. He was good to me, though. During this period I was staying with him and he picked up the tab for food and all my other expenses. In the end the concert was not the success he had hoped for. I felt so sorry for him. He went through a lot of anxiety and stress trying to resuscitate his career and it was a bitter disappointment to fail.

I was in for yet another disappointment myself. The one thing that Goldkette had been able to negotiate for me under our personal management deal was a job as a staff singer doing sustaining (non-sponsored) broadcasts on NBC. It was a great opportunity, and I was very excited at the wide exposure that it promised. I was scheduled to start in early September. On September 3, 1939, war was declared between England and Germany and all sustaining broadcasts were pulled off the air. It seemed that even Hitler was trying to screw up my career!

Nothing was going right for me. Bandleader Mitchell Ayres, who later worked with Perry Como, decided he liked my singing but turned me down cold after an audition at the St. George Hotel in Brooklyn. He thought we looked too much alike, and didn't want to confuse his audience!

I went back to scuffling until May, 1940, when I managed to land a job as an M.C. on a luxury cruise to South America. I thought that this was pretty heady stuff, and I immediately started to get ready and wrote home to tell my parents. They wrote back and told me that my little brother Sam, who wasn't so little any more, was planning to tie the knot next month. I was delighted for him, and came home to serve as best man on June 2, 1940.

While in Chicago a bone spur that I had developed on my knee began to rub against the muscle and the scraping caused it to swell. It was very painful, and I ended up having to undergo surgery to set things right. The operation required a lengthy recuperation during which I couldn't move around much. Because of this, I "missed the boat" on my South American cruise.

After all the other setbacks I'd faced these past few years, I began to doubt that my ship would ever come in.

One of my happy times.

FOUR

BLACK AND BLUE

Soon after my knee got better and I was able to get around again, I received a card from Art Cutlip that gave me someplace to go. "Come on back to Cleveland," he wrote, "I'm working here and I'm working there and together we can start all over again." He was in the process of setting up a gig for us at the Sterling Hotel. By the time I'd managed to hitchhike my way back to Cleveland, however, Art had decided that I wasn't going to make it and accepted a teaching job. I was stranded in Cleveland again, with just enough money to last me the week.

I was preparing to thumb my way back to Chicago when I ran across a girl named Drusilla who'd been a waitress at Lindsey's Sky Bar when I was working there with Art. She thought her roommate, Betty Green, could probably get me a job at a place where she'd been singing called the College Inn. It was a hangout for the kids from nearby Fenn College. They came in to eat chicken in a basket, guzzle beer, and enjoy the live entertainment at night. I went down there and sang and the boss offered me a job and twenty bucks a week. Things were so loosely organized that he had me emcee the shows my first night!

The very next morning I got a call from Ray Raysor, another piano player and good friend of mine who had played for me around Cleveland. He said that there was a great girl singer just in from Detroit, and I had to help her because she was starving. I pleaded that I had just found work myself and hadn't seen dollar one yet, but Ray insisted that I take a listen and sent her down to the club that night.

I was on the stand when she came in and waved to me, so I waved back and motioned for her to take a seat. When I finished I came down and asked if she was hungry, knowing all too well from personal experience that that was the most important question. The answer was yes, but she wanted to wait until after she'd sung. I said O.K. and went back on the stand and gave her a big introduction: "Ladies and Gentlemen, I have a very happy surprise for you. A good friend of mine, one of the finest singers in the country, has just come in from Detroit. She's one of the nicest gals I've ever met in my life, and I'd like for all of you to meet her now. June Hart!"

Now, of course, I'd only just met her and had never heard her sing before in my life. I was just going by what Ray Raysor had told me, though she was a tall, slim girl with great square shoulders and really looked to me like she could give out with a song. As it turned out, I didn't regret a word of my introduction. She was fabulous.

Her style was reminiscent of Mildred Bailey, and she left the stand to tremendous applause. The boss came running around and demanded her name. She told him and he said, "You want to work here? I'll give you thirty-five bucks a week." She was ecstatic and I was very happy for her, but I must confess it nettled me to see her hired for fifteen dollars a week more than I was getting. Afterwards when we sat down to eat she asked me if I thought that thirty-five was all right, and when I admitted that I was only making twenty she thought I was kidding.

This began to prey on my mind and the next night I couldn't help but corner the boss and ask him about the difference in salary. He pointed at June who was seated at the bar and said, "She's going to be able to drink it back. You don't drink." This was true enough, but it still struck me as damned weak reasoning. The boss could sense my discontent, and he didn't want any disgruntled employees. He solved the problem by firing me. I was let go with four days' wages, a colossal eleven bucks.

When June found out what had happened she wanted to quit too, but I talked her out of it. There was no sense in both of us being out of work. I couldn't afford the little room I had taken any longer, so she offered to let me move in with her at the Mount Royal Hotel, a local show business hangout. I slept on the couch for a week and a half, and during this time I got to know her pretty well. We had the same musical rapport that I'd shared with Art Cutlip, and her repertoire consisted of the jazz standards and ballads that I loved so much. We would talk about music into the early morning hours and I was fascinated that we had both been so strongly influenced by the same people. June took the tender blues approach of Mildred Bailey, and she also loved Billie Holiday. I had just seen Billie Holiday work for the first time on my last trip to New York, and no other singer (with the exception of Louis Armstrong) has ever had such a profound effect on me.

I'll never forget listening to Billie at a club called Kelly's Stables on 51st Street. The place really had been a stable many years before, an old brewery where they used to keep draft horses to haul around the drays. She had that big trademark gardenia in her hair, and accompanying her was the Nat King Cole Trio. While Armstrong had won me over with his improvisation and the rhythmic drive of his playing, Billie was the master stylist and mood setter whose vocal interpretations were just stunning. I really picked up a lot from listening to her over the years.

Back in Cleveland, I started picking up a few things by listening to June Hart. I may have been fired, but the College Inn was a public place and they couldn't keep me out of the joint. I used to go hear her every night, and I was especially taken with one "oldie" in her repertoire. It was an obscure little 1931 ballad entitled *That's My Desire*. I though it was very pretty, and the melody spent a long time running through my head before it burst out in spectacular fashion a few years later. After her show, June would pick up the tab for our food and beer. I was still as broke as could be.

Meanwhile, a friend of mine named Bill Furman had fallen in love with a girl singer named Linda Keene who was working with bandleader Red Norvo at the Trianon Ballroom. They decided to elope, and Norvo was going crazy with no girl singer. I went down to see him and introduced myself. "I've been working at the College Inn with a girl named June Hart," I told him, "and I don't know if I'm saying a good or a bad thing here, but she sings just like Mildred Bailey." Mildred and Red had been married and used to work together, but she stopped singing with him after they were divorced. Red said he'd like to hear her, so we went down after hours to listen to June at another place called the Cabin Club. He thought she was great and decided to take her with him to New York. This marked the beginning of what has been a long and dear friendship between Red and me, but at the time it also meant the end of my meal ticket. I had no idea where to turn next.

Cleveland was a great jazz town in those days, and I'd met a lot of the local talent by going around to the different afternoon jam sessions. Many musicians used to congregate at a place called the "Chateau" something or other,

At a disc jockey interview in St. Louis, with my arm
around Percy Faith.

where the comedian was a brash youngster named Joey
Bishop. One guy I met, a piano player named Kenny
Rasmussen, got me an audition at a little joint he was
working in called the Wonder Bar, across the street from
the Palace Theater. Thank goodness they hired me. It not
only provided a livelihood for about six weeks, but it gave
me an opportunity to work out and refine with Kenny the
book of songs I had assembled with Art Cutlip.

During this time Pee Wee Hunt played the Palace
Theater. He was a wonderful trombone player and singer
who was riding high at the moment because some of the
records his little group had made, like *Small Fry*, were
doing extremely well. The Wonder Bar was next to the
theater, and every night his sidemen would troop out of
the stage door and come across the street to where I was
singing. I began to nurse the hope that Pee Wee might hear
me and take me with him, which never happened. We did

meet and become friendly, though, and when I told him about my book of songs he said, "Gee, I'd sure love to see that." I loaned it to him and that was the end of my book. I never saw it again. Pee Wee left town, and a few weeks later the Wonder Bar folded.

* * * * * *

I'd like to be able to tell you that I never gave up on singing, that all the setbacks I faced never fazed me in the slightest, but that just isn't true. After the loss of my songbook and the closing of the Wonder Bar, I was pretty disgusted. I thoroughly enjoyed Jack Teagarden's recording of *Black and Blue*, not only because he was such a fine singer but because it pretty well summed up the way I felt after toughing it out all these years for nothing. In February of 1941 I threw in the towel and decided to find some steady work.

One of the customers at the Wonder Bar, a guy named John Curley, was a plant foreman at the Parker Appliance Company, where they made airplane parts like tubes and hydraulic fittings and then shipped them to California for assembly. He used to drink his fair share and often requested me to sing his favorite songs for him when he was in his cups. Then he would leave late at night to work the midnight to 8:00 am shift at the plant. When he found out the joint was closing down, he asked me what I was going to do next. It looked like I'd have to head back to Chicago again. "You know, Frank," he said, "we're making awfully big money down at the plant. It looks like the war is going to become a vital concern real soon." I decided that steady work might be a welcome change of pace and became a semi-skilled machinist. When I received my first paycheck for $150, I thought, "To hell with singing!" but that was my head and not my heart talking.

I worked the midnight to 8:00 am graveyard shift, and when I felt like vocalizing I shouted my head off and no one could hear me over the clatter and roar of the machinery. My interest in music remained strong, and one night on the job when a phrase popped into my head I decided to turn my hand to songwriting. Within the hour I had finished my first tune, *It Only Happens Once*. Songwriting was a way of keeping in tenuous touch with my first love, and I played with it over the next two and a half years. In the meantime, Pearl Harbor had happened and the country was at war. I tried to enlist in both the Army and the Navy, but they classified me as 2B and wouldn't take me because my occupation was considered vital to the war effort. Failing an "audition" with the draft board was almost too much for my pride!

The graveyard shift at the plant left me with a lot of free time during the day, and one afternoon I was flipping around the radio dial when I came across a group that absolutely floored me. They were three women (I'll just call them "The Girl Trio," for reasons that will become clearer later), and I heard them singing on radio station WHK. A drummer friend of mine from the Cabin Club, Morey Feld, happened to be working their broadcasts, and he invited me to visit the station.

The following day I showed up and was introduced to the girls and got to see them perform. The lead singer, Linda, was just incredible. She sang New Orleans-style jazz with a tremendous flair. After the show I walked up to Morey and said, "These gals are great! What the hell are they doing on a radio station in Cleveland?" "They won't be here for long," he told me, "they just got a call from Johnny Mercer to go out on the Coast and record for Capitol Records." Capitol was a new company at the time, but I was still very impressed.

I got friendly with the girls and they told me about their plans over dinner. Then we went back to their apartment and swapped our life stories, and it turned out that they'd been scrambling for a long time in the same way I had.

During the next couple weeks we grew very close and a romance blossomed between Linda and me. One of the girls was married to a fellow named Arnie Freeman, who had been serving as their temporary manager, but he'd been called up by the Army. They didn't want to go out to California without management. Linda started talking about how nice it would be if I went along and took care of them.

I began nosing around and trying to figure out how I might get transferred to a new plant the company happened to be opening up in California to speed production and save on freight charges. Luckily, most of the guys were married and owned homes and didn't want to give up the security of their lives in Cleveland. All the spare manpower was being drained by the military, and "Rosie the Riveter" and many other women were being called on to handle the big machines. I screwed up my courage and took hat in hand to the second floor, where we menials down below never went, and blurted, "Who do I see about a job in California?" Soon I was getting tires and gas stamps and loading up a 1938 Pontiac for the trip West. I drove through Chicago to pick up my little sister Rose for company, and in August of 1943 we were off to California.

* * * * * *

Rose quickly grew homesick and left me to fend for myself in a little apartment on the corner of Las Palmas and Hollywood Boulevard. I had been all over the Eastern Seaboard, but never west of Chicago before '43, so it took me about a week to get acclimated. I wanted to live in Hollywood, but the plant I was transferred to, Pacific Screw Products, was in South Gate. This left me with a sixty-four mile daily commute, and to make matters worse I really wasn't qualified for my new job at the plant. Luckily they gave me the graveyard shift again, from five in the afternoon until five in the morning, and the fellow that did my job during the day broke me in. I would sleep from seven in the morning until one in the afternoon, and then I'd have three free hours before returning to the grind at the plant.

I spent the majority of that time on Vine Street where I met the whole range of actors: musicians, radio people, eccentrics, and hangers-on that used to flood that area in those days. I was mainly interested in establishing some contacts for The Girl Trio, who had come to Hollywood ahead of me and were getting ready to record with Johnny Mercer. We used to see each other nearly every day and discuss our plans for the future. Things between Linda and me progressed to the point that she was wearing an engagement ring that had belonged to my mother.

I arranged for them to audition for Sammy Lewis, a Beverly Hills impresario, and got them a job at Slapsy Maxie's, a big and popular nightclub on Wilshire Boulevard. Sammy also owned a club in San Francisco, and rather than open them in L.A., he sent the girls up north first to break in their act. They scored a tremendous success in Frisco, just as their first record was about to be released. When they got back to Los Angeles, The Girl Trio no longer wanted to be bothered with me and refused to accept my phone calls.

I didn't have my first hit record until I was 34, after seventeen years of trying. That kind of struggle helps you to put success, when and if it comes, in the proper perspective. The faintest glimmer of achievement, however, seemed to give Linda a terminal case of what I've come to describe as "the big-time attitude." When she finally deigned to see me she was aloof, arrogant, and as cold as ice.

Our farewell scene was played out in a parked car, and as far as she was concerned there was nothing left to discuss. She got out, tossed my ring onto the seat beside me and walked out of my life. I felt stunned and so churned up inside that I leaned out the car door, certain I was going to vomit. The nausea passed, however, the same way my broken heart healed, with time.

It may take all kinds to make a world go around, but there are certain types you're better off without.

FIVE

CARL

At least The Girl Trio provided me with an excuse to move to Hollywood, something I had been planning to do for a long time. Pickings had been pretty lean back East, in Chicago, and in Cleveland, so I didn't have much to lose by starting all over again in California. Why not storm the entertainment capitol of the world? I was hoping that the hard times had bottomed out in New York.

Early in my stay I learned that MGM was holding auditions for their all-male chorus, so I went over to Culver City and tried out for a lady named Kay Thompson. I did a jazz tune for her and she liked what she heard. As part of the chorus I sang background music in *The Harvey Girls* and a few other musicals. Kay remembered my audition and would use me when a number called for a jazz treatment. In the Danny Kaye picture *The Kid From Brooklyn*, there's a sequence where a fat guy is dancing with Vera Ellen and he sings about eight bars of music. Well, that was my voice. I've recorded seven theme songs for films since then, mostly Westerns, but I suppose you could say that was my first movie soundtrack!

In September of 1943 I learned that Nat King Cole was in town, playing with his King Cole Trio at the 331 Club on 8th Avenue. Nat was then enjoying his first flush of success, but he wasn't yet so big as to be unapproachable. I went down to the club and caught him at an afternoon rehearsal. I introduced myself and told him about *It Only Happens Once* (the song I'd written while working in the Cleveland defense plant), which I felt was a pretty good tune. Nat became interested enough to record the number for MacGregor Transcriptions, but his rendition ended up languishing in the vaults for many years (although it has recently resurfaced on compact disc). Our meeting, however, marked the beginning of my long and rewarding friendship with a great talent and one of the nicest persons I've met in show business. Nat was a warm, deep, sensitive musician, and it's funny to think back now that his ballad stylings were often considered "white" for a black man, while mine were "black" for a white singer.

Among all the different people I encountered during this period, there was one fellow whose friendship and support helped my career more than any other. His name was Al Jarvis, and he was a Los Angeles disc jockey who enjoyed tremendous influence and popularity. If Al plugged your record you were in, and he could just as easily kill it. We met while I was still running around town trying to get The Girl Trio some air time for their first release.

Al used to organize troupes of entertainers to visit the various military hospitals in California. I told him I was interested and in October of 1944, after breaking off with The Girl Trio, I started to go along on Sundays (my only day off from the defense plant). We must have hit every hospital in California with a one day, up-and-back bus trip. On my first trip we visited Port Hueneme, a Seabee base in Oxnard, and performed in front of 6,000 raucous guys in a big hall. I was nervous as hell, not knowing what to expect from this sort of audience. I sang *Baby, That Ain't*

Right, which I had learned from listening to Nat Cole's record (although my version also incorporated a few bars of a blues I heard Billy Eckstine perform while he was with Earl Hines). The guys went crazy and stomped and yelled for "more blues!" I didn't have anything else prepared, so I started improvising new lyrics to the same music! I sang whatever words came to mind and the men loved it. After a few more shows Al started giving me some M.C. duties and I became a kind of right hand man to him.

Usually our settings were much more intimate than the big hall in Port Hueneme. At places like Hoff General Hospital in Santa Barbara, we'd just wheel a piano around into the different wards and perform for small groups at a time. Our personnel kept changing, but usually there would be a few musicians, singers, maybe a comedian and the occasional added attraction. You'll never guess who turned up on a trip to Palm Springs to play a hospital that used to be located where the El Mirador Hotel stands today. The Girl Trio.

It goes without saying that I wanted nothing to do with them. We didn't talk to each other or even look at each other, and when the time came for their introduction I skipped the build-up and presented them with the fewest words I could get away with (six): "Here they are, The Girl Trio." I didn't sound very enthusiastic. Al noticed that I wasn't my usual self with these girls around and when we got back to Los Angeles he asked me about it. I told him the whole sorry story. Al and I had become pretty close and friendly by this time, and he was outraged at the way they'd treated me. He put a hand on my shoulder and said with icy finality, "Frank, I'll never play their lousy record again." He never did.

As I mentioned earlier, in those days if Al Jarvis didn't play your record in L.A. you were dead. I don't think that the girls, Johnny Mercer, or Capitol Records ever knew what happened. The Girl Trio was undeniably talented,

At the Morocco with Al Jarvis, (left) and Woody Herman.

After success, a return visit to Hoff General Hospital in
Santa Barbara.

and I really believe that at one time they had an excellent opportunity for tremendous success. After that show in Palm Springs, I never saw or heard of them again.

* * * * * *

On one of those bus rides back from a hospital I sat down next to a very pretty little blonde girl named Ursula McGowan. I'd noticed that she didn't perform during these shows, but instead went around to the different beds and comforted the patients, talking and passing out cigarettes and gum and things. She complimented me on the show I'd just done and told me that she was trying to break into the movies and the modeling world. We started talking about show business, and she asked, "Do you ever write songs?" I told her about the one that I'd done back in Cleveland. It turned out that she had a friend whose collaborator had just gone into the Army and he was searching all over for a new lyric writer to work with. This would be something new and different, and it sounded exciting. I let Ursula know that I'd be very interested in meeting her friend. He was in the maritime service on Catalina Island playing piano for, of all bandleaders, Ted Weems. He had a ten-day furlough coming up, and so through Ursula I arranged for all of us to meet on the following Monday afternoon at a Nat Cole rehearsal.

I'll always remember my first encounter with Carl Fischer. Nothing particularly momentous or unusual happened, but we'd barely exchanged greetings and clasped hands before I sensed that this man would be important to my life. How right I was! For the next ten years Carl was my friend, partner, and musical inspiration. Of course, I couldn't have foreseen all that at the time. But I did know that this tall, spare Cherokee Indian with a pencil-thin mustache and a million dollar smile was somebody special.

After Ursula left us, Carl suggested that we go over to his house to be near his piano and all his music. There I met his wife Terry, who made coffee and sandwiches while we swapped our life stories. Then Carl handed me a thick sheaf of music and said, "Gee, Frank, I hope you can get these done in a hurry. I've got to get back in ten days." Carl and his previous collaborator, Bill Carey, already had *Who Wouldn't Love You?* and a few other successful pop tunes under their belt, so I cautioned him that collaborating was all new to me. He asked if I read music, which I did, but I couldn't write down the notation. "That'll be my department," replied Carl, and we settled down to work.

Before Carl left for Catalina, he played a melody for me on a demonstration record that was hauntingly unforgettable. It took me six months to come up with the words for it. The result was *We'll Be Together Again*, a song that has been recorded by over 100 different artists (See Appendix III), even though it got off to a shaky start. Carl and I had a lot of trouble placing both *We'll Be Together Again* and *It Only Happens Once* with a music publisher (eventually we formed our own firm, Foremost Music). We finally found a New York publisher, Bregman, Vocco and Conn, that liked both tunes. Unfortunately, they dissolved eight months after accepting them. The Pied Pipers made a recording of *Together*, however, and that proved to be the first inkling of the success that was finally beginning to trickle my way.

In the meantime, May of 1945, the end of the war was finally in sight and I was let go from my job at the defense plant. Without that steady income I had a lot of trouble swinging the rent on an apartment. For a while things were nip and tuck and I ended up moving around frequently. Then one afternoon Al Jarvis asked me where I was staying and I explained my situation. He said that he was living alone at the plush Garden of Allah, and generously suggested that I move in with him. It didn't seem that we would be getting in each other's way much. He was working days at the radio station and I was out most nights making the rounds of the jazz clubs. The offer was a godsend and I took him up on it.

The Garden of Allah was considered to be a very snooty address in those days. It was quite a fashionable place and many celebrities lived there. Perry Como was across the courtyard from us, Woody Herman was next to him, and Robert Benchley was just a few doors down They had a gorgeous swimming pool and I spent many pleasant afternoons by its side. One day I was watching a little kid fool around when suddenly he fell in. He looked to me to be struggling, so I dove in and yanked him out. I remembered all too well the time when the same thing had happened to me at the altar boy picnic. The kid turned out to be Perry Como's son, Ronnie. Later, when Perry thanked me, I was glad I had a chance to return the kindness he'd shown in getting me that job back in 1937.

Al Jarvis was the person who helped me land my next job. He dreamed up the idea for a group called the Make Believe Ballroom Four, featuring Slim Gaillard on guitar, Winnie Beatty on piano, Ray Ramone on drums, and Billy Hadnott on bass. I handled the vocal chores. Al featured us live three times a week on fifteen-minute radio broadcasts over station KFWB. He was one of the only disc jockeys in the world at that time to occasionally feature live music on his broadcasts. We were on the air with Jarvis for over a year. I should mention here that by this time all my experiences and my various musical influences and passions had really come together. I was singing in the style that I later became well known for. I've often been referred to as the first of the "belters," but that's a catch phrase that I don't like because it's not accurate and doesn't mean much. I was just trying to emphasize the rhythmic aspects of the songs I sang, using my voice the way a jazz soloist uses his instrument. "Crooning" may have been the more commercial style, but it wasn't for me.

We weren't getting any money for the broadcasts, so Al arranged for us to audition for a paying job at the Swing Club on Hollywood Boulevard at Las Palmas. It was just up the street from the hotel I'd first checked into after coming West from Cleveland. The owner hired us for three months, and between those shows and the radio work a lot of people around town were hearing me sing.

On our fourth day at the Swing Club a young kid with a saxophone walked up to the bandstand and asked, "Who's the leader?" I asked him what he wanted and he said, "I'd like to sit in." I told him to get his horn out and he proceeded to blow everybody right out of the joint. He was a bit young, but so fantastically talented that we hired him on the spot. Unfortunately, Stan Getz wasn't with us a week before somebody found out he was only sixteen and underage. They yanked him off the bandstand. In all the years since that time, I only crossed paths with Stan again once. For years we'd just miss each other while touring in different towns. We started leaving messages behind, and it became something of a joke. Then one afternoon in the mid-'60s at the Toronto airport, we bumped into each other while he was getting on a plane and I was getting off. We barely had time to shake hands, much less reminisce. It was a great loss for music when he passed away in 1991.

After closing at the Swing Club, the Make Believe Ballroom Four landed a job at a steak house in Glendale for another two weeks. Then work became scarce and the group broke up. All the time that we were together, Slim Gaillard had been working on his own very individual routine of songs and comedy patter. Between (and during!) numbers he used to ramble in a crazy mixture of phony Latin and slang phrases that was way ahead of its time. He'd only throw an intelligible word into every other sentence, but somehow you always understood him and his act was very funny. He had earlier teamed up with bassist Slam Stewart ("Slim & Slam") in New York, and they achieved some pretty fair successes with records like *Flat Foot Floogie*. After that act broke up, Slim joined forces with bassist Tiny Brown. The two of them auditioned around town and eventually landed a job at Billy Berg's on Vine Street.

Billy Berg's was a hot little jazz nightclub where a lot of musicians used to hang out (it was also one of the only clubs in the area at that time that used to welcome black customers). I started hanging around the Sunday afternoon jam sessions held there, where I first met Duke Ellington, Art Tatum, and many other legends. While at Berg's Slim made a few records (including his best known song, a novelty entitled *Cement Mixer, Put-ti Put-ti*) for a small company and they really caught on. Everybody from NBC and CBS, which were nearby, came in to hear this new guy at Billy Berg's. Slim became a very popular attraction. I went to see him and every night, out of gratitude for his stint with the Make Believe Ballroom Four, he'd call me up to sing. When he began to develop a following (and we knew that the customers might grumble if I cut into his time), I started singing with a new group that followed him into Billy Berg's called Milton Delugg and his Swing Wing. You never knew who was going to turn up in those clubs and I hoped that if the right person heard me something might happen.

March 5, 1946, is another one of those dates that I won't soon forget. I was on my way to Billy Berg's when two rough looking characters held me up. Actually, they must have been beginners because they were shaking worse than I was. In my wallet sat the last forty bucks I had in the world. I tried to explain this to them, but I should have saved my breath. "That's forty more bucks than we got, pal. Hand it over!," was their response. The next night when I showed up at Billy Berg's my total net worth was exactly thirty-nine cents.

I tried to put it all out of my mind while singing, and later in the evening I was doing my old favorite, *Rocking Chair*, when somebody in the audience stood up and started trying to shush the crowd so he could hear the music better. I didn't have my glasses on and had no idea who it was. When I finished he came around to the edge of the stage and it turned out to be none other than the song's composer, Hoagy Carmichael. He asked my name and wanted to know where I was working, which was nowhere at the moment. I was pleasantly stunned that he would even bother to take an interest in me. Hoagy led me over to Billy Berg and said, "Why don't you put this kid to work? He sings great." Billy replied, "What for? He comes in every night and sings for nothing!" We all laughed and the upshot of it was that Billy hired me for $75 a week as an intermission singer.

Billy Berg was quite a character. He liked to play gin rummy all night with a couple of his cronies in the back room, even though there were nightly remote radio broadcasts from the club that he was supposed to host. When he found out that I was good friends with Al Jarvis and had done live shows on KFWB, Billy took me aside and said, "Look, Frank, I'm in the middle of a hot gin game. Why don't *you* do the broadcast tonight?" He cared about the show's success, but he didn't give a damn about being the M.C. himself and pretty soon it was my job. All this was great exposure for me, but it's hard to make ends meet on great exposure and seventy-five bucks a week.

To help supplement my meager income, I took up a pastime that's proved both rewarding and frustrating over the years. I spent many of my days hanging out at another Vine Street place called the Key Club. The Key Club was full of horseplayers. One afternoon, like a classic sucker, I asked Don Raye and Gene DePaul (the songwriting team responsible for *Cow-Cow Boogie* and *I Remember April*) about those mysterious charts they had spread out all over the tables. Before I knew it, I was hooked. I went out and bought every tip sheet and newspaper I could lay my hands on to study. I discovered that a handicapper for the *Los Angeles Herald-Examiner*, Maurice Bernard, was the best in town. You could usually count on him for at least a couple of winners a day. I worked out a progressive betting system based on his picks that everybody at the Key Club scoffed at. It wasn't one hundred percent reliable, of course, but I'll tell you that it did help pay a few bills. Regrettably, I've never found a handicapper since (I sadly include myself) as reliable as old Maurice Bernard.

* * * * * *

One afternoon I headed over to a place called the Suzy Q to hear Erroll Garner. At the time, he was a great new pianist who'd just hit town from Pittsburgh and everyone was talking about him. It was a bright, sunny day and when I walked into the dimness of the club it took me a minute or two to adjust to the lack of light. I didn't need my eyes, however, to appreciate the fact that there was a *storm* coming from the piano. Somebody was playing his butt off! It didn't sound like what I'd been hearing on records, though. Erroll Garner had a very distinctive, late left hand style, and this sounded like whoever was playing was all over the keyboard. When my eyes adjusted I saw that it was a kid who didn't look a day over fifteen.

Immediately, the wheels started turning in my mind. I'd been in the business long enough to know that nothing is for certain and to realize that I might never make it as a singer. My limited success promoting The Girl Trio left me feeling that I might instead have some potential as a manager. I went up to the kid and introduced myself and asked his name. "Andre Previn," he replied.

"Where do you work, Andre?"

"Nowhere. I'm still in school."

"Who's your manager?"

"Nobody."

"Well, is there somebody I can talk to? I'd like to try and do something with you."

"Like what?"

"I'd like to be your manager."

That brief exchange left me very excited, because I sensed a great opportunity here. Andre took me over to a table where his father was sitting and we all got acquainted. His parents were Polish immigrants who'd managed to get out just before their country was clobbered by Germany.

Andre said, "Well, I'll be in school for a couple of more years and then I'll wait and see what happens. But in the meantime, do you know Duke Ellington?" It turned out that Andre and his father both idolized Duke, whom I had in fact met earlier at Billy Berg's. Duke Ellington was every bit as suave and elegant as his music. (The easiest song lyrics I ever wrote were to a tune of his that became *What Am I Here For?* I set them to paper at Billy Berg's, but didn't submit them for Duke's approval until he guested on my television show eleven years later).

He was due back at Berg's the following Sunday afternoon, so I had Andre and his father meet me there. I told Duke that I wanted him to meet one of the greatest piano players in the world, and he arched his eyebrows in that bemused way of his and replied, "Oh, really?" Even though he was about to go on stage, Duke smiled graciously and sat down and charmed Andre and his father for five or ten minutes. They, in turn, were very impressed that I was able to arrange this little get together.

I phoned Al Jarvis to tell him about my discovery, and he mentioned that Nat Cole was going to be his guest in the studio the next day. Al was largely responsible for Nat's early success, and he suggested that my "boy wonder" might want to come down and meet another great pianist. Andre met me at KFWB after school the following day. I hadn't warned him and he was just stunned to see Nat Cole sitting at a microphone talking with Jarvis. Al had very slyly set up two pianos back to back in the studio, and after the introductions he said, "I think it would be a memorable occasion if sometime in his future Andre could look back and say that he'd played the piano with Nat Cole." Nat really didn't know what to expect, but they hadn't been playing for very long before his eyes got big as saucers. They jammed together for ten minutes and Andre was absolutely incredible.

Two weeks later the same thing happened again at KFWB with Eddie Heywood, who had come to town to play at Billy Berg's. He was one of the big names in instrumental music. Eddie had scored with a hit version of *Begin the Beguine*, and he later did even better with *Canadian Sunset*. Andre's playing left him slack-jawed and dumbfounded. I was in pretty solid with Andre after taking him to meet all these great people.

We went over to his house to have a serious talk with his folks. I explained who I was and told them about my "many contacts" in the entertainment business. I mentioned managing The Girl Trio and said we'd split after a disagreement. The fact that the girls had recorded for Capitol, however, left Andre's parents with the impression that maybe I could do something for him. "Now, I realize that he's still in school," I told them, "but the minute he leaves I'd like to sit down and get serious with you."

Things didn't work out that way. I don't know whether it was through that little bit of exposure that he got with Al Jarvis or something else, but somehow word about this prodigious talent filtered back to MGM (It might have been through Charles Previn, Andre's uncle, who worked in the music department at Universal and, coincidentally, scored a few of my wife Nan's films there). Almost before he was out of high school somebody from the studio signed Andre up and he started scoring pictures. You all know the rest of the story. I may have lost a management client, but the world of classical music gained a genius.

Looking back, it's clear that this was all for the best. If I had been a success at managing Andre Previn I probably would have gone into that field and never made my mark as a vocalist. In fact, the two of us first met when I was finally on the verge of breaking through.

I started at Billy Berg's on March 6, 1946, and on March 18 Carl Fischer was medically discharged from the service and we were able to begin working more closely together. I was still scraping to get by, but at last a few decent breaks had come my way and I had a reassuring sense that success was at least a vague possibility in the future.

I couldn't have known that in a very short time a simple little song from my past would dramatically change the course of my life forever.

Frankie and Carl Fischer at Opening at Ciro's Club, 1950.

With a very young Andre Previn and actress Phyllis Kirk
at Ciros, 1951.

With Carl, drummer Morey Feld, and Connie Haines.

SIX

THAT'S MY DESIRE

After leaving Billy Berg's, Milton Delugg and his Swing Wing got a contract to cut four sides for Mercury Records. This wasn't surprising, because the Swing Wing was a seven-man group that was loaded with talent: Herman Saunders on piano (he went on to become the executive producer for many of Jack Webb's T.V. Shows); Tony Rizzi on guitar; Lou Paine (an exceptionally good drummer); Bob Manning on bass; and Abe Most on clarinet (Abe was later hired by Time-Life Records to recreate many of the classic clarinet solos from the Big Band era). Milton Delugg, who went on to do a lot of television and movie work in Hollywood, played a swing accordion (talk about a rare talent!). At the time Milt was a protege of Frank Loesser (the songwriter), and the stint at Berg's had led to a recording contract.

This fine ensemble was without a vocalist, so Milt asked me if I'd like to do two songs at the session (the other two sides were strictly instrumentals). I accepted and got my hopes up again, although I'd been in a recording studio twice before with less than spectacular results. In 1944 a guy named Dick Elwell really liked the way I sang and set up a fledgling little company called Beltone Records. We made one single of a song called *In the Wee Small Hours of the Morning* (it was an up-tempo blues, not the later Sinatra song of the same name) backed with a wartime tune entitled *Brother, That's Liberty*. The record didn't go anywhere and Beltone went bust. The masters were later acquired and re-released by the Gold Seal label, and have since become a real collector's item.

My next effort on wax was very unusual. I was approached by Robert Scherman, who owned the Atlas Records label. He had recorded Nat Cole before Nat hit it big and moved to Capitol. Bob offered me $50 a side to cut two singles in the style of the King Cole Trio. So I imitated Nat on two songs, *Melancholy Madeline* and *Maureen*. The former sold over 100,000 copies in the New York area. Everyone just assumed that Nat had released these records under an alias (we had a fair facsimile of his sound going and even featured Nat's trio guitarist, Oscar Moore, on both sides). This time I sold records, but I had to imitate somebody else to do it. Later, to fulfill contractual obligations, I cut sixteen more songs for Atlas. They were mostly old standards like *Moonlight in Vermont* and *Roses of Picardy*, but this time I sang them my own way.

To get back to Milton DeLugg, I was cut down to one song when somebody came up with the idea of saving money by sharing studio time with a radio comedian named Artie Auerbach. Auerbach used to be featured on the Jack Benny show, playing a character named Mr. Kitzel who spoke in an ethnic, high-pitched and silly style (his catch phrase was "Could be!"). Milt had worked up an arrangement of a novelty number featuring this character called *Pickle in the Middle With the Mustard on Top*. When we got into the studio, Auerback was absolutely petrified at the thought of recording a song. It frankly amazed me to see someone who was used to doing his stuff live for millions of listeners freeze up at the sight of a studio microphone, where you can do something over and over again until you get it right.

The *Pickle* song was set in an amusement park, and I was given the chore of providing atmosphere by shouting "Peanuts! Popcorn! Get your red hots!" in the background. I kept time by lightly tapping on Auerbach's shoulder to help him with his entrances. He took so many takes to get it right that by the time he and Milt were both finished we had three minutes left in the studio. I had one take on my song and that was it. If I couldn't get it right the first time, I wasn't going to be on the session. Fortunately, I already knew the song I wanted to do and there was really no need for rehearsal because the Swing Wing and I had already performed it together dozens of times at Billy Berg's. I recorded *I May Be Wrong But I Think You're Wonderful,* and Mercury put it out as the B-side of *Pickle in the Middle.*

As soon as I could lay my hands on the record I took it over to Al Jarvis for his opinion. "What kind of chance have I got against a song like this?" I asked him, and played the A-side featuring Mr. Kitzel. Al rolled his eyes and said, "That's a horrible piece of material. Don't worry, I'll concentrate on *I May Be Wrong.*" When Al started playing my record, the floodgates finally broke open. People called in and wanted to know about this new singer, and the company trying to promote the Milton DeLugg records kept getting requests for "F. Lane [sic]," which was the way I'd been credited on the label. Mercury Records back in Chicago began to take notice of the fact that they had a fair sized regional hit on their hands, and Los Angeles was an important market.

Now I was really getting started, but I hadn't yet arrived. It's funny: a familiar song like *I May Be Wrong* opened the door for me, but it took an oldie that nearly everyone had forgotten to finally seal my success.

* * * * * *

Even though my record was doing well I was still considered just an intermission act at Billy Berg's, someone whose short sets consisted of standard songs that were hard to hear over the rattle of dishes and the rumble of disinterested conversation. People were beginning to trickle in requesting *I May Be Wrong*, however, and I felt confident and comfortable to the point where I decided to take a few chances.

One evening I was sitting in the club shooting the breeze with Edgar Hayes, who had come into Billy Berg's with his trio, The Stardusters, after the Swing Wing left (Edgar had recorded one of the first hit instrumental versions of *Stardust* back in 1931). I made it a habit to come in to work early, and Edgar did too, because he was commuting from Riverside and never knew what the traffic would be like. In the few hours before the first set at nine o'clock we could rehearse or try out new things. On this particular evening we had just finished having dinner together and over coffee I asked him about a thought that popped into my head out of nowhere. I said, "Ed, do you remember a song called *That's My Desire*?"

Ever since my experiences with June Hart back in Cleveland at the College Inn that ballad had been prowling around my subconscious. June sang it in her act, and you might say that I *absorbed* it rather then learned it. I wasn't too sure of the lyrics and I wasn't too sure of the melody. Fortunately, Edgar was fifty-five years old and had been around long enough to remember this obscure tune that was first published in 1931. If I had been talking to a younger man I probably would have received a blank stare in response to my question and dropped the subject.

But Edgar leaned back and smiled and said, "Oh yeah, that's a pretty one. It would be a good song for you."

"Do you think we might try it tonight?" I asked him immediately.

He nodded and after we'd finished our coffee we went over to the piano to run through it. "You do the verse?" Edgar asked as he sat down. I didn't even know there was a verse. "That's all right," he said, "don't fool with it." We went through the song twice and I thought I had it. "That's close enough," said Edgar.

I waited until the heart of the evening and my eleven o'clock set, which was the most important one because it was the last set before the remote broadcast. I asked for a drum role and waited until the place quieted down before I made a little speech that changed my life:

Ladies and Gentlemen, I have an important announcement to make. I know that I'm just an intermission performer who sings you a few standards to fill the gaps between star attractions here at Billy Berg's. Sometimes you pay attention to me and sometimes you don't. I've been here for quite a while and I've been very content to just sing the same old stuff up until now. Tonight, however, I've got something special for you. Tonight I've got a brand new song. . .

I turned to Edgar and asked him to play *That's My Desire*. He was giving me a peculiar look, because he really didn't understand that big build-up. As far as he was concerned we were just rehashing an old tune. The audience, who had probably expected my announcement to be about a car blocking the driveway, was genuinely interested. I had their undivided attention as I launched into the lyric:

To spend one night with you
In our old rendezvous
And reminisce with you
That's my desire

To meet where gypsies play
Down in that dim cafe
And dance till break of day
That's my desire

We'll sip a little glass of wine
I'll gaze into your eyes divine
I'll feel the touch of your lips
Pressing on mine

To hear you whisper low
Just when it's time to go
Cherie, I love you so
That's my desire

When I finished the place just erupted. The smile on Edgar Hayes's face took me back to Jess Stacy and the Merry Garden Ballroom all those many long, hard years ago. "Frank, you've got a hit!" he exclaimed. "Ed," I protested, "it's not a record." He waved his arm over the crowd and said, "Well it's sure as hell a hit in this room!"

Mrs. Berg, a former Rockette at Radio City Music Hall who worked in the place as head waitress, came running to the foot of the stage and said, "Frank, that's one of the most beautiful songs I ever heard. Sing it again!" I ended up singing *That's My Desire* **five** times that night, and each time it was a smash.

I really can't tell you why I chose to bring up that particular song with Edgar on that particular night, or why I went out of my way for an attention grabbing, big introduction. All I know is that within weeks that song had built to the point where I was the star attraction at Billy Berg's, and every night they had to turn people away. This coupled with the success of *I May Be Wrong* finally added up to too much for the record companies to ignore.

At the urging of his children Milt Krasny, an agent with the General Artists' Corporation, came down to Billy Berg's to see what the fuss was all about. They lived at the Garden of Allah, and one of his kids recognized my name as the guy who had taught them how to dive in the swimming pool. Milt came down, liked what he heard and loved what he saw in terms of the enthusiastic crowds. After the show he sat me down and asked me how I'd like to cut four sides for Mercury Records.

Mercury was a relatively young company in 1946, and though I had no idea at the time, they were on the verge of going under before my first few records hit it big. They had Eddie Howard, Tony Martin, and (later) Vic Damone on their roster but they just weren't boasting tremendous sales. They'd also recently signed a girl singer for whom they hadn't yet discovered the right combination of musical elements. The company later asked Carl and me for our opinion of her, and we both agreed that she was fantastic and was bound to make it big sooner or later. Her name was Patti Page.

All things considered, it was the sort of recording opportunity I'd always dreamed of. I told Krasny that I'd love to do it and he asked me what songs I might like to try. *Desire* had to be one of them, and after that I didn't really care what they picked.

Apparently my insistence on one particular song rubbed Mercury's A & R man (artists and repertoire), Berle Adams, the wrong way. He sent back a telegram from Chicago that said, in effect, "no way in hell is *he* going to tell *us* what to record." Well, *Desire* had carried me too far for me to abandon it now. I laid it out plain and simple: Either I recorded *Desire* or I didn't record. Period.

I think my reckless stubbornness must have surprised Berle Adams quite a bit. If I was willing to gamble on the rest of my career for the sake of a song, he realized that it must be a whale of a tune and asked to see a copy of the sheet music. Now I was really stuck. Not only had I never seen one, I had no idea where to find one. I didn't know who published it, who wrote it or anything. I asked around and finally located a store in Hollywood called Ring Music that specialized in old sheet music. The guy who ran the place told me flat out that, "I only have one copy and you ain't going to buy it." He charged me a dollar to sit down in the store and copy out the words and music by hand. I took that with me over to the music library at KFWB, which had featured a broadcast orchestra at one time. I asked the librarian if he had a score copy or some musical instrument part to a song called *That's My Desire*. He found a violin copy that had the melody but no lyrics. Now I had an authentic melody that coincided with the melody on the sheet music, but to my surprise it bore little resemblance to what I'd been singing at Billy Berg's.

I suppose you'd have to call my version an "improvisation on the original," but then that's really what jazz is all about anyway. At the time I couldn't explain it that way and kept thinking, "Oh Christ, what am I going to do now?" I decided that I had to stand my ground with Berle Adams. I sent him the music as I'd copied it along with a note which read, "This song I have to do. You can pick the rest." After a tense wait he sent me a return telegram: "OK. *Desire* is a great song. You pick the rest!" The ironic thing is that every one of the more than two dozen cover versions which quickly followed on the heels of my record all copied my improvised arrangement, so none of us really had it right! (After my version clicked the publisher changed the sheet music, added my name to it, and gave me a third of the copyright to share with songwriters Helmy Kresa and Carroll Loveday. Kresa, by the way, was for many years Irving Berlin's right hand man and the first person to see many of his compositions.)

I decided that I also wanted to record *By the River Saint Marie* and *September in the Rain*. To placate the record company I rounded out my four sides with a song that they'd suggested, a blues entitled *Ain't That Just Like a Woman*. Strangely enough, although it wasn't a big hit for me, it turned out to be my father's favorite song of everything I've ever recorded.

Nervous anxiety kept me awake the entire night before we went into the studio. On the morning of September 15, 1946, I found myself in the Radio Recorders' studio on Santa Monica Boulevard in Hollywood, along with Carl Fischer and Mannie Klein's All-Stars (featuring Mannie on trumpet, Don Bonne on clarinet, Phil Stevens on bass, George Van Eps on guitar, and Lou Singer on drums). We recorded *Desire* at 9:00 am. After we were finished I wanted Carl's thoughts on how it went. He was happy for me but seemed a little distracted, and when I asked him why, he told me the sad news that he'd kept to himself for the length of the session: his father had passed away earlier that morning.

* * * * * *

Desire was finally released on December 15. Now that, of course, "'tis the season to be jolly," and at first the record was lost amidst all the Christmas music. Al Jarvis, however, was kind enough to play the hell out of it in the Los Angeles area and pretty soon Billy Berg's was packing in four hundred people a night. This prompted Billy to give me a big, twenty-five dollars a week raise.

In early 1947 the record began to catch on nationally in a very unusual way. In those days *Billboard* magazine carried Harlem charts as well as pop charts. The Harlem charts — Harlem New York, Harlem Chicago, Harlem Los Angeles, etc. — were supposed to reflect the tastes of black record buyers. *Desire* was the number one record on all these charts before it ever appeared on a pop chart.

This didn't surprise me. In my leaner days I failed many an audition because, I was told, I sounded "too black." My manager later had heated arguments with disc jockeys across the country who refused to believe I was a white singer. Even my future wife Nan thought I was black when she first heard me on the radio. I'm certain the confusion was the direct result of the music that influenced me while I was developing my style. I guess I became the first of the so-called blue-eyed soul singers. That's why it irks me a little nowadays to hear Elvis Presley touted as "the first white man who sang black." I had to scuffle for seventeen years because I "sang black."

This confusion over my background also prompted an incident which sheds an interesting light on the flip side of racism. I was in Detroit visiting the record shop of Sid Dickler, a good friend of mine who supplied the discs for juke boxes all over town. We were chatting when a large, jovial black fellow came in to pick up a batch of the latest Frankie Laine releases for his machines in the black sections of town. He obviously didn't know who I was, and I went along with the gag and discussed myself in the third person. At one point, he nudged me in the ribs and said, "That brother sure can sing!" Sid told him that Frankie Laine was white, and he became belligerent. When I settled things by proving who I was, he stormed out of the place dumbfounded. He also cancelled his standing order for my records.

Another interesting thing about *Desire* was that it caught on abroad before it hit in America. Mercury had no international distribution outlets in those days, but some V-discs of the songs were pressed and shipped to the troops in Europe. A disc jockey named Ralph Snyder in Munich, Germany, started playing the record like crazy over the Armed Forces Radio Network. That's how the British record buying public, who have been so good to me over the years, first heard my voice.

Back in the States a Philadelphia disc jockey named Eddie Hurst picked up on the record and really started plugging it on station WPEN. In L.A., Gene Norman followed Jarvis' cue and pushed it at station KFWB. Eddie Hurst later confided to me that the song helped bring him and his wife together. Countless other couples over the years have told me the same thing. By February of 1947 I was really riding high.

Before the record charted, an old school chum of mine from Lane Technical High School back in Chicago named Sam Lutz approached me about becoming my personal manager. His agency already handled Lawrence Welk and a few others. I knew that I was going to need a good manager very soon, but I had to explain to Sam that I couldn't afford one on the money I was making at Billy Berg's. "No problem, Frank," he insisted. He marched up to Billy Berg, demanded an additional twenty-five dollar a week raise, and promptly got me fired.

I went right through the ceiling. Everything was finally falling into place and now I didn't have a job again. "Don't worry," Sam reassured me, "we're moving two blocks up the street to a place called the Morocco." The Morocco was a slightly larger club, and at the time they were featuring the great Red Nichols and his Five Pennies. Red was happy for my success and when I came in for rehearsal he was anxious to see my arrangements. I'd never worked with arrangements. I just told the guys at Billy Berg's the song and the key and away we'd go. Red was insistent. "Frank, you've got to have arrangements!" he said. As a personal favor, at no charge, he had his clarinetist (Heine Beau) write me four great small band arrangements for *Georgia On My Mind* (one of my first big records after *Desire*); *Black and Blue, On The Sunny Side of the Street*, and *I'm in the Mood for Love*. Those songs and *Desire* were the extent of my repertoire at the Morocco. Thank goodness we had a turnover every show, because I kept singing the same songs over and over all night long!

At the risk of sounding immodest, I must admit the Morocco was doing incredible business. I opened the day after Thanksgiving in 1946 (before the record was out), and even with four shows a night you couldn't get a seat in the joint. Every night it was the same story. Mondays were just like Saturdays, and the place sat 600 people. They even started charging admission, which was unheard of in the small clubs at the time, and at sixty cents a head the crowds just kept getting bigger. My salary started at $150 a week and was raised fifty bucks each month. Before I left the Morocco after nine months, *Desire* was the number three record in the country.

After the record hit the charts in February, Mercury flew me out to Chicago to be featured at the National American Music Merchants Convention. It was my first trip in an airplane, and my first appearance outside of California after gaining some recognition. They put me up at a plush downtown hotel, the Continental, and I floored everybody at a convention party with an hour-long show featuring *Desire* and a host of other songs reaching all the way back to my days in Cleveland with Art Cutlip.

It was during this trip to Chicago that I was fixed up with a hairpiece for the first time in my life. I'd been thinning on top for a long time, and my management decided that a singer needed a full head of hair to appeal to the kids who bought records. I hated the damn thing. The first night I had it on, I was scheduled for a publicity interview with Dave Garroway, who was the top radio personality in Chicago in those days. I glued it on with a strip of spirit gum, but I didn't do a very good job. As soon as I stepped out of the hotel the wind whipped it off my head and it went rolling down the street like a tumble-weed. Sam Lutz went chasing after it while I stood at the door to the cab, cursing a blue streak.

What Sam finally brought back had been run over a few times and looked pretty pathetic. I refused to wear it. I didn't feel like going back to my room to get the acetone to remove the spirit gum, either, so I scraped it off in the back of the cab. At the interview, Garroway never made eye contact with me once. He spent the entire hour staring at the red line across the top of my forehead. These are some of the joys of wearing a hairpiece. (Many years later during an engagement at the Copa, I was signing an autograph for a lady at a ringside table who wanted a better look at my face and tried to lift me up by the hair. You can guess the rest.)

So much was happening so fast in 1947 that I hardly knew whether I was coming or going. Even after waiting for so long, I was unprepared for most of it. Sam Lutz helped by assembling many of the things I needed but didn't have, like publicity photos and a stage wardrobe. Next I had to get a full time accompanist/arranger, but that didn't take long. I knew it could only be one person. Carl Fischer had been keeping busy playing piano for Pee Wee Hunt (the guy who left Cleveland with my songbook in tow), and had in fact been largely responsible for the success of Pee Wee's biggest hit, *Twelfth Street Rag*. Carl took over the conducting and arranging duties from Red Nichols and joined me at the Morocco on June 15 (three years later I got married on that same date).

After eight months at the Morocco I was ready to move on, but they were making so much money that nobody wanted me to leave. I stayed on for another month and then left in July and urged them to hire Kay Starr as my replacement. She had done a great job substituting for me in April when I was laid low for a couple of weeks by some minor surgery. Later, on my recommendation, Berle Adams (the A & R man who didn't want me to pick my own material, and who'd earlier represented Louis Jordan) became Kay's personal manager.

In August I got an offer from the Million Dollar Theater in Downtown Los Angeles. They booked me, Dave Barry (a comedian who later became a big name in Las Vegas), and the Ike Carpenter Orchestra. Together we did seven shows a day, and my paycheck finally began to reflect all the years of hard work. At the end of my last week at the Morocco I was paid $750. After my first week at the Million Dollar Theater, they handed me a check for $11,700. I'd never seen so much money before. If I had, it belonged to somebody else!

The funny thing about that figure is that when I was small and daydreamed about great riches, the way poor children so often do, the "fantastic sum" of eleven thousand dollars always entered into my mind as representing all the money in the world. That amount was soon dwarfed by my first royalty payment for *That's My Desire*, a check for $36,000. The day before I'd recorded the song I was seven thousand dollars in debt. I desperately needed to get a sense of perspective on all this, so I asked Carl to come into my dressing room for a serious discussion.

For the first few minutes we just sat and looked at that check, looked at each other, and cried. I finally broke the silence. "Carl, if I'm going to be capable of earning this kind of money we have to decide something right now. How long can this last? Am I going to be around for a while or should we milk this for all we can before it sputters out?"

Carl was a stoic and usually kept his innermost feelings to himself, but he was a very sincere man and every once in a while he'd get a look in his eye that told me he'd overcome his natural reserve and was speaking from the heart. He had that look as he leaned toward me and put an arm around my shoulders.

"Frank," he said softly, "from what I hear every night, from what I see in their faces when you sing, you've got a big chance to go all the way for as long as you want to go."

SEVEN

COMING BACK ON A WHITE HORSE

I've always found it amusing how a little success can change the way people see you. During my run at the Morocco, the King of Swing himself came up to congratulate me on my show and tell me that I was wonderful. I'd first met him a long time before, during my scuffling period, and he held quite a different opinion of my talents back in those days.

In August of 1942 Don Haynes, a friend of mine who covered the Cleveland area for *Downbeat* magazine, drove me from Cleveland to Cedar Lake, Ohio, for an audition he'd arranged with Benny Goodman. I did *Wrap Your Troubles in Dreams* and a couple of rhythm tunes. Benny listened patiently then said, "I want a *ballad* singer. The girls sing the rhythm things with my orchestra." I tried to convince him that I could handle ballads as well, but he said I just didn't sound up to them. I later heard him grumbling to somebody, "Look what they're bringing to me to listen to these days . . ."

At least Benny was reasonably polite. Back in Chicago in 1937 another bandleader, Eddie Duchin, personally promised me an audition and then had me thrown out when I showed up backstage at the theater. I don't know if he'd had a bad show or maybe a rough time the night before, but Duchin insisted he didn't remember me and when I persisted he bawled me out with some salty language and saw to it that I got the bum's rush. In 1948 he came in to see me at the Harem (which later became Bop City) in New York, and this time he was all smiles and accolades. Neither he nor Goodman realized that they'd ever seen me before. I didn't bring up the past or try and rub the rejections in their faces because there's nothing to be gained with that sort of behavior. Their new outlooks, however, were a sure sign that I'd finally arrived.

A third bandleader, Woody Herman, also dropped by the Morroco and liked what he heard. I'd never dealt with him professionally, but we had been neighbors for a short time when I was rooming with Al Jarvis at the Garden of Allah. After the show Woody told me, "Frank, you should be singing in New York. You've got to play the Paramount." I was in awe of the Paramount Theater. Bing Crosby, Frank Sinatra, and Perry Como had all used it as a major step in their rise to superstardom. I didn't think I was ready, but Woody insisted and he called up Bob Weitman, who later became a Hollywood producer, and Bob Shapiro, who managed the Paramount at that time, and arranged a December booking for me.

Before that engagement, I warmed up with a lot of traveling. I was anxious to get out and perform and meet the people who were buying my records. My first date outside of Los Angeles after *Desire* hit was at a place in San Francisco called Harry Greenbach's Burma Bar, and during the two weeks there we broke the town wide open. I'd never seen such enthusiastic fans. From there it was on to Saint Louis, Philadelphia, Chicago, Detroit, Boston, and eventually up north to Canada. The cities that I visited on my first tour have proved to be among the kindest to me over the years, and I always look forward to returning to them.

In October of 1947 I took some time off from the road to get back to Hollywood and record my first album and a few extra singles. Albums were a brand new thing back then, usually consisting of three ten-inch records with a song on each side. Every song on that album, called *Frankie Laine Sings*, was a familiar old standard. We had no choice. The Musician's Union was preparing to go on strike against all the record companies, and the deadline was December 31. The demand for studio time and good session musicians was incredible. We were lucky to have the chance to make the album in the first place, so I made it a point to choose songs that wouldn't need much work and that everyone would be familiar with: *Black and Blue, Wrap Your Troubles in Dreams, Blue Turning Grey Over You, I Can't Believe That You're in Love With Me, West End Blues* (a sentimental choice), and *On the Sunny Side of the Street.* The musicians handled them easily, but the sessions were still hectic.

Jimmy Hilliard, who was then our A & R man at Mercury records, booked some recording time at Universal Studios. We ended up in a little room on the second floor that was very hard to find. Some musicians had to get up in the middle of things and leave because they were booked for another session, and many of them had still another commitment after that! Carl sat at the piano, frantically trying to scratch out little parts for all the guys who came and went. Our tenor sax man, Babe Russin, had to go while we were still left with two hours of studio time. We wanted to get Vido Musso (a big band stalwart who for years played sax with Benny Goodman, Harry James and Stan Kenton) to replace him, but he got lost trying to find the right studio. Luckily our drummer, Lou Singer, happened to have his vibes with him. When we were ready to record *Black and Blue*, he took the solo on his vibes that would normally have gone to the sax player. Today that solo is considered a classic, much talked about by jazz buffs as one of the great vibes performances.

In December 1947 came the engagement at the New York Paramount that Woody Herman had helped set up for me. I was still reluctant to shoulder the entire responsibility for the success or failure of the show, so I went in as the "sub-headliner." Top billing went to Billy DeWolfe, a comic who had a riotous stage act which he performed in drag. I was trying to hedge my bets with DeWolfe, but it was pretty apparent that the people were coming in to hear me. By this time every record store on Broadway was playing *That's My Desire* over their loudspeakers. My next couple of releases, *A Sunday Kind of Love* and *Mam'selle* had followed *Desire* right up the charts. The timing was perfect and we enjoyed a tremendously successful stay at the Paramount. A lucky one, too. We ended our run on December 21, and on the 23rd New York was hit by one of the worst winter storms in its history.

Though it sounds corny now, back in 1937 I promised myself that I wouldn't come back to New York unless I could do so "on a white horse." I'd reached my lowest point of despair in that town, and I couldn't forget the nights spent sleeping in Central Park and the days that dragged by without food. That's why I made it a point to treat myself to one very special evening during my first run at the Paramount. I spent it alone. I donned a custom made suit and a camel's hair overcoat and headed for Central Park. There, I sought out the dilapidated bench that had once been my bed. I sat down and ate a candy bar and thought about the time when penny candy bars were all I could afford to eat. In one of my pockets sat a loaded wallet, in the other a key to one of the most comfortable hotel suites in town. After a while I hailed a taxi and drove

Receiving a popularity award with Jo Stafford from DJ Peter Potter, 1947. We later recorded many duets together at Columbia.

The first time I worked the Paramount, December '42.

to the heart of Times Square, where my name was in big, beautiful lights and they were paying me $2500 a week to do what I loved best.

I only hope that everybody, at least once in their lives, knows such a moment.

* * * * * *

I was back on the road after the Paramount and in January of 1948 I had a memorable experience while playing a place called the Palomar in Vancouver, Canada. I was doing a special show for teenagers, and for a buck they got admission and a glass of Coke. In the middle of the proceedings a young black fellow clambered onto the stage and announced, "Hey, I do a great impression of you!" Well, the audience wanted to hear it and so did I, so I let him have the stage for a while and he was terrific. Afterwards I gave him a big congratulatory handshake and the crowd applauded like crazy. Later, I found out the kid's name: Sammy Davis, Jr.

I worked my way back to Los Angeles and my first hotel circuit stint at the Cocoanut Grove in July of 1948. I was very proud to have my mother and father at a ringside table on opening night. Shortly after the money started rolling in, I retired Pa and bought him and Ma a nice house in Burbank. The whole family moved out West for a time, though not everybody chose to stay (eventually my brothers Sam and Joe went to work for me as promotion men for my records, Sam doing most of the traveling and Joe working out of the offices we set up in Los Angeles).

On July 25 I was changing clothes backstage at the Cocoanut Grove when someone sent a note to my dressing room saying there was a certain lady who wanted to meet me. It was her birthday, and for her present she'd asked to be taken to our show. Apparently she'd flipped the first time she heard *That's My Desire* on the radio. When I came out to meet her, it was my turn to flip.

I didn't need any introduction. I recognized her right away as Nan Grey, an actress who had caught my eye back in 1936 when I saw her with Deanna Durbin in *Three Smart Girls*. She was so pretty that I'd been daydreaming about her ever since. To my delight, our personalities clicked and we hit it off with each other immediately. We talked the night away, but the hectic treadmill I was on prevented us from getting together again for some time. It wasn't too long after that second meeting that the romance began to snowball, leading to our marriage in 1950.

Back at Mercury Records, I was about to embark on what might be described as a "musical marriage." After the October 1947 recording session, Jimmie Hilliard left Mercury and with the new year I found myself confronted with a new A & R man I'd never met or heard of before. We wouldn't get to work together for a while, either, because the strike prevented us from recording any new material. Fortunately, the stuff released from the first album session was doing very well. *Shine*, which I'd recorded at that time, became one of the biggest songs in the country and stayed on the charts for nearly thirty-five weeks, which helped carry us through the strike. This left plenty of time to get to know the new kid on the block. His name was Mitch Miller.

Before coming to Mercury, Mitch's background had been strictly classical. He was considered one of the top oboists in the world, and was associated with the Rochester Symphony and the Eastman School of Music. When I learned all this I grimaced and thought, "Christ, what's a guy like this going to do for me?!" When we finally met, we got along great. He was a mischievous character and a great storyteller. Mitch was smart, too. He realized just how much he didn't know about this new business he found himself in, and was eager for advice.

93

Mitch was able to use the entire strike year of 1948 to learn his job. I sort of took him by the hand and promised, "I'll tell you all I know, which ain't a helluva lot." I'd only been recording for less than two years at this point, but three of my first five releases (*Desire*, *Shine*, and *Two Loves Have I*) had sold a million copies, and to sell a million records in those days was quite a stunt. To a degree, he had to respect my judgment.

My advice was just common sense. I told him to study his singers and emphasize the type of material he felt they handled best. Offer them their kind of songs, then if the singer turns you down you're off the hook, and if he or she has a great success with your recommendation you're a hero. We ended up enjoying a long string of successes together, and from the start Mitch demonstrated a talent for setting off voices in original, if not downright quirky, musical settings. Who else would've put a harpsichord on a Rosemary Clooney record, or backed Guy Mitchell with swooping French horns? In my voice he said he detected a kind of "universal quality" to communicate meaning. He successfully pushed me into new directions that I would never have explored otherwise. Mitch also got along great with Carl Fischer, and understood what he meant to me musically.

Late in '48 he decided that he wanted to try and sneak in our first session. We were in Newark, New Jersey, and everything had to be kept hush-hush because technically we were breaking the strike. We cut six jazz-oriented sides, among them *Rosetta*. They're very rare records today. The personnel is a bit fuzzy in my mind, but I do remember we had the great trumpeter Cootie Williams on loan from Duke Ellington. The songs were good ones, and it's too bad the session took place under such adverse conditions. Also, my throat was raw from overwork. I'd been on the road too much and hadn't yet learned how to pace myself. I sang like every note was going to be my last. In a few years this abuse caught up with me in a very painful way and I lost my voice for a while. At this time, however, after a little rest it was usually as good as ever.

Mitch and I settled down to work in earnest in April of 1949. The recording strike had ended in January, but I was on the road until March. Mitch had been familiarizing himself with my sound, and he sent me a song that he thought would be right. "I hear this as a combination of *Old Man River* and *Black and Blue*," he told me. I took it over to Carl's house, told him what Mitch had said, and we listened to it together. We could hear a weariness that echoed *Old Man River*, but this tune was nothing like *Black and Blue*. It wasn't jazz at all. Instead, it had a Western flavor to it. The title was *That Lucky Old Sun*. I knew it was a change of pace for me, but it was such a fantastic song that I decided it would be a good way to begin our association.

In the meantime, I had picked out fifteen other songs for myself that I thought had good potential. *Fifteen other songs*. We went into the studio for four nights straight and recorded four of them each night. These were very important sessions, too, because people were wondering, "What's Laine going to come up with next?" It turned out that I could just as well have passed on fourteen of the fifteen songs I'd chosen. They were good tunes, but nothing happened with them. The only piece of material that I came up with that had the potential to be another big song was a thing called *I Get Sentimental Over Nothing (Imagine How I Feel About You)*. Where did it wind up? Lost on the back of *Lucky Old Sun*! That record was released in August, and in three weeks it was the number one song in the country.

I decided that if I could goof fifteen songs in a row, and Mitch could come up roses on his first shot, then he deserved a pretty big say in things. He reminded me that I'd done pretty well before he came along, so we agreed

With Mitch Miller.

Disc Jockey Bob McLaughlin presents Doris Day and me with a popularity award. We enjoyed a hit duet together with *Sugarbush*.

A visit from songwriter Jimmy McHugh, the man behind
On The Sunny Side Of The Street.

A "Jam Session."

to collaborate in finding songs. Before I could come up with my first suggestion, Mitch brought me four million sellers in a row.

* * * * * *

If it hadn't been for the success of *Lucky Old Sun*, I never would have accepted the next song Mitch brought to me. In September of 1949 I was in Minneapolis when Mitch called me from New York. He was very excited. He said he'd found my next big record, and he played the song for me over the phone. I listened, and I couldn't believe what I heard. When Mitch got back on the phone I said, "Jesus Christ, you can't expect me to do a *cowboy song*! I'll lose all my jazz fans. I'll lose everybody who ever loved *That's My Desire, Sunday Kind of Love, Shine* and *Mam'selle*. I won't do it!" Mitch tried to reason with me and used his "universality" argument. "Frank, I've listened to you, I've studied your records, and I know what you're capable of doing. You can do any song that anybody hands you if you make up your mind to do it. Now, let me play it for you again."

I listened again and still wasn't impressed. If *Lucky Old Sun* hadn't done so well I would've turned him down cold. I felt I owed him one, however, even at the risk of disorienting my fans. I've always thought of myself as primarily a jazz singer, though over the years country and gospel influences have crept in. Regardless of the type of material, I've always tried to sneak in a little jazz somewhere. A lot of critics don't think of me as a jazz singer, but I believe that's primarily because I've been successful with pop tunes. You can be the jazziest singer in the world, but once you start to sell records you've "gone commercial."

To get back to the story, I finally gave in to Mitch and asked him where he wanted to meet to record the song. It had to be on a Sunday, because I was closing in Minneapolis on Saturday and opening in Detroit on Monday. We agreed to meet in Chicago and Carl and I flew in around noon and met Mitch at the publishing office. Carl looked over the material we were supposed to record, and I could tell that he sided with me. "I'll just have to do the best I can with it," he grumbled.

When we got to the studio and began working on it, we found that the more we played with this tune, the more interesting it became. The more fun we had with it. We didn't have an arrangement worked out, but when all the necessary people showed up we started feeling our way through. Morey Feld (my old drummer friend from Cleveland days) had joined me, and Mitch called in the Art Van Damme Quartette and a singing group called the Mello-Larks. While Carl was making last minute scribbly notations on the music and the engineer was getting all the mikes and balances properly set, I was sitting in the middle of the studio trying to figure out what the hell I was going to do with this number. Mitch walked up to me, slapped me on the back and said, "Frank, this song is going to revolutionize your life, the same way *Lucky Old Sun* did." I could only sit and shake my head. "I don't know Mitch, I just don't know. It doesn't sound to me like the type of thing I should be doing, but if you think I should sing a song called *Mule Train*, I'll do it."

There was one big technical hitch we had to overcome to make the record. We needed a reasonable facsimile of the sound of a whip crack. I had a lot of trouble with my throat in Detroit the following week, because instead of resting my voice on my day off I ended up singing *Mule Train* all afternoon. We couldn't get that damn whip crack right! We must have had four great takes, except for the whip, and we tried everything. First the drummer hit a rim shot, then he whacked the top of a barstool, then somebody took off their leather belt and started waving it around in the air. Nothing worked. I think part of the problem is that we knew what was really making the sound.

99

If you see someone make a sound by whacking a bar stool, then *that's* what you think it sounds like, not like somebody cracking a whip.

Finally, after about the tenth take, I turned to Mitch in desperation and said, "Isn't there a sound effects library somewhere for shows like *Death Valley Days* with the sound of a whip crack in it that you can just dub in later?" That's what we finally did. We made one last take, and during the whip crack parts everybody kept silent. Later, Mitch went up to the soundtrack music library and dubbed in the whip (I've seen it written that Mitch was actually cracking a real bullwhip in the studio while I was singing. That's a hell of a mental picture, but it's not true).

A week later, they sent me a copy of the record in Detroit. It surpassed my wildest expectations. On Saturday night, closing night, I had the sound man cue it up on the theater's sound system, which was used to play music in between performances. In those days I was closing my shows with *Shine*, which happened to be particularly popular in Detroit (it sold over 100,000 copies there). Just before I got to *Shine*, though, I walked to the edge of the stage and told them that I had a surprise.

I said that I'd just received an advance copy of a record that would absolutely stun them, and I gave them the choice of hearing it or letting me end with my usual closing number. Naturally, everybody started hollering "Play it!" so I cued the soundman and sat down by the footlights. Once again I experienced one of those special moments where the power of a song just fills the room with electricity. The audience was cheering so hard when the record ended that there was no point in doing *Shine*, but I couldn't just walk off the stage after playing a record. My last song was just a grace note and when I finished all I heard were shouts of "Play that record again!" I knew I had another million seller on my hands.

Back in Los Angeles, I couldn't wait to get the record to Al Jarvis. I didn't want him to know that anyone else had heard it first, so I had my publicity man, Red Doff (who helped make widespread my new nickname, "Mr. Rhythm"), pull a fast one. He went over to KLAC, where Al was working at the time, and burst into the broadcast booth pretending to be out of breath. He said he'd just swiped a copy of my latest record off my desk, and he wanted Al to play it quickly before I found out and got peeved. With a grin Al lifted the needle off of a recording of Ralph Flannigan and his band playing *Gianinamia* and put on *Mule Train* unannounced. When it finished, the switchboard lit up like the proverbial Christmas tree.

Now, unbeknownst to me, Vaughn Monroe, Gordon MacRae, and Tennessee Ernie Ford had already recorded this song. Their versions were all still sitting in the can without a release date set. When their company executives heard that my recording of *Mule Train* was on the radio, they had copies of their versions in Al's hands in about fifteen minutes. In the interest of fairness, Al decided to promote a spontaneous *Mule Train* contest. He kept playing all of our versions over and over again, and asked his listeners to call in and vote for their favorites. When Al went off the air three hours later, well over a thousand phone calls had poured in and I'd come up the winner.

Mule Train has become a song that's widely identified with me now, and I can't get away without including it in my shows. I've been blessed over the years with the ability to put a very individual stamp on certain songs and make them my own. That's why the cover records of *Desire* by more established artists didn't do as well as mine, and why I think I managed to pull out ahead of the *Mule Train* pack, though I should note that there was one more fellow who took a crack at it.

The first thing in the morning after the radio contest, Decca Records had Bing Crosby in the studio recording *Mule Train*. They backed it with *Dear Hearts and Gentle People*, and Decca brought the full force of their corporate power and the prestige of the Crosby name to put pressure on Mercury. My version was released a week before Bing's and that, coupled with the fact that *Lucky Old Sun* was sitting at number one, proved enough to give me an edge. *Mule Train* zoomed up to number two on the charts, and after a while it swapped places with *Lucky Old Sun* and they held that way for a couple of months.

To my great relief, even Bing Crosby didn't catch that.

Album cover, *Hell Bent For Leather*, 1961.

With Bing Crosby at the Desert Inn in Las Vegas.

A family reunion at my parents' 50th Wedding Anniversary.
From left: Sam, Gloria, Joe, Pa, me, Ma, John, Rose, and Phil.

With Irving Berlin and Jimmy Durante.

EIGHT

NAN

In 1948 I played my first of many singing engagements in Las Vegas. The desert air has proved hard on many singers, but the salaries are usually too tempting to pass up. In 1949 I returned and followed Joe E. Lewis into the El Rancho. This took me back many years to the memory of another job that had been indirectly connected with Joe. He was a barbering client of my father's back in Chicago, and during my Merry Garden Ballroom period Pa had prevailed upon Joe to get me a job as a singing waiter at a place called the Royal Frolics. My first customer was an old curmudgeon who made me so nervous that I accidentally spilt a huge bowl of soup over his head and got canned!

1949 also brought my first trip to a movie studio. After a brief appearance in a film called *Make Believe Ballroom*, I went over to Columbia for my first featured role in a musical. The picture was called *When You're Smiling*, and the most memorable thing connected with it happened to me off camera. Al Jolson was also at Columbia filming his life story, and during a break he visited our set. I finally got to meet the man who'd inspired me to sing profession-

Meeting my childhood idol, Al Jolson, at Columbia in 1949.

The cast of The **Big Show** broadcast, Dec. 17, 1950. Front, left to right, Louis Armstrong, Tallulah Bankhead, Deborah Kerr. Back row, left to right, Jerrry Lewis, Dean Martin, Bob Hope, Meredith Wilson, and Frankie Laine.

ally, and he proved to be a warm, wonderful personality. We took a picture together which I still treasure to this day.

I was told that when Jolson first heard *That's My Desire* on the radio, he called Al Jarvis to find out who was singing. Al told him that it was his roommate, and Jolson said, "That guy is one of the best singers to come down the pike in a long while. He's going to put all of us old-timers out of business!" Praise like that from the likes of Jolson meant the world to me. Many stories have been written since then that make out Jolson to be a cold and rude egotist who often snubbed fellow performers. I only know that the gentleman I met was gregarious, likable, and kind.

Back at Mercury, Mitch Miller brought me a song he felt we should use as the follow-up to *Mule Train*. It was called *The Cry of the Wild Goose* and had been written by a guy named Terry Gilkyson, who ended up providing me with a lot of quality material over the years. Terry was a society lad from an "old money" Philadelphia family, loaded with loot, but all he wanted to do was sing and write folk songs (he later had his own sizable hit with a calypso song called *Marianne*). Because of scheduling problems, I couldn't get to New York to record the song and Mitch couldn't make it to the Coast. Instead, he recorded the music track in New York and sent it out so I could overdub it. This was my first experience with overdubbing, which you weren't supposed to do according to the Musician's Union. I liked being able to listen to the backing first and then think over my performance before recording. It wasn't too long after the January 1950 release that we had another million seller.

Goose was the fourth million seller in a row which Mitch brought to me in the incredibly short space of six months. After *Mule Train*, we'd found another big hit in *Swamp Girl*, a very offbeat song by a writer of specialty material named Michael Brown. It was all about a Lorelei of the marshes who lured men there to meet their doom, and it was out of line with anything I'd been doing up to that time. It still sounds avant-garde today. Latching on to unusual material became a regular strategy. We were always trying to come up with the unexpected.

A lot of the offbeat stuff did have a common thread, though. *The Cry of the Wild Goose* was essentially a folk song, and I think that you can argue that *Mule Train* and *Swamp Girl* both fit into the same category. Nowadays when they talk about who started bringing folk music to popularity, a lot of people cite the Kingston Trio and *Tom Dooley*. I think that was really pseudo-folk, like *Goose* and *Mule Train*. After all, genuine folk songs are usually one or two hundred years old. Those songs that Mitch brought me helped spark interest in folk music years before the Kingston Trio ever saw their first pair of Bermuda shorts. The only difference is that their stuff was presented explicitly as folk music, while my releases were always considered "pop" song stylings. The new waters we were testing out brought in offers from all over the world.

While touring in April of 1949, I ran across Nan again in an owner's box at the Golden Gate Park racetrack in San Francisco. This was nearly a year after I'd first met her at the Cocoanut Grove, but our relationship picked up right where we'd left off. Soon I made it a point of asking her out whenever we were in town together. We liked to return to the Grove as often as possible and one night, while dancing to *Blue Moon* (our special song), I confessed my deep feeling for her and our romance really blossomed. This was definitely love and we knew we wanted to get married, but we had to wait out a divorce proceeding that Nan had been involved in when we first met (she'd been married to a well-known jockey, Jackie Westrope). We finally tied the knot in an unpretentious ceremony on June 15, 1950. Nan's two daughters from her previous marriage, Pamela and Jan, might just as well have been my own. They've been a great source of pride and pleasure to me over the years. Family has always been important to me. I was a little overwhelmed to have my own all at once. Success meant that much more to me now that I had someone special to share it with.

Nan is an incurable traveler, like me, and we had a memorable South American honeymoon together. I managed to pick up some lovely Portuguese songs while in Rio, and some Spanish stuff in Argentina (years later I wrote and recorded a jazz samba called *Nan*). All went smoothly until Nan suffered a minor case of appendicitis that laid her low and we had to head back home to Encino. In 1953 we moved to Beverly Hills, into a big, comfortable house that once belonged to silent movie star Richard Dix.

After we returned from our honeymoon and Nan felt better, I went into Ciro's on Sunset Boulevard for an extended engagement. We had a wild opening night. In those days I used to bring an actual bullwhip on stage with me for *Mule Train*. Milton Berle spontaneously decided to join me on stage, and he grabbed the whip out of my hand and started cracking it at everybody. We had a lot of fun. It was also during this run at Ciro's that a song came into the office that absolutely knocked my ears back. If ever a tune had "HIT RECORD" written all over it, this was the one. Carl agreed, but it turned out we had to sit on the song for nearly nine months.

My contract with Mercury was up in March of 1951, and I would've been perfectly happy to renew except for the fact that Mitch Miller had left the label to take over Mannie Sachs's job as the head A & R man at Columbia Records. He had opened up so many new vistas for me that I didn't want to break up the partnership, but I felt an obligation to Mercury. Their guys started dropping hints about picking up the option long before it was due. I also had to consider the fact that I couldn't re-record anything that I'd done for Mercury until at least five years after I'd left it.

At the wedding with Dick Gabbe, Sammy Lehrer (maid of honor), Seymour Heller, Sam Lutz, Pam and Jan.

Leaving for our honeymoon.

At our Beverly Hills home that once belonged to actor Richard Dix.

At Sardis, picking up a few tips on grooming from Duke Ellington. (Note the chopsticks.)

Mitch understood my dilemma, and reassured me that if Mercury didn't come up with an equitable deal there would always be a place for me at Columbia. I decided to wait for the Mercury brass to approach me, because I didn't want the company to think that I was anxious or in an awkward position. When talks began with my manager, Sam Lutz, we relayed their offer to Mitch and he decided that he could indeed get us a much better deal.

Sam managed to secure some wonderful guarantees from Columbia. In addition to a minimum annual salary regardless of record sales and one of the first deferred royalty payment plans (this helped out a lot with taxes in the days of the ninety-percent bracket. These days it's almost a standard arrangement for singers.), he got them to come up with $50,000 to finance a half-hour kinescoped (which is what they used to call taping in those days) pilot for a television variety program.

I met in Miami with Irv Green, who was then the President of Mercury Records, to give him first refusal and a chance to match Columbia's offer. I was sorry to put him on the spot, and stressed that there wouldn't have been a problem if Mitch hadn't left. Irv said that he was unable to come up with anything comparable to what Columbia had laid on the table, but if I would make a couple of albums for him before I left the label then I could do so with his blessing. I figured that was getting off easy, and in a way I was sad to see my stay at Mercury end.

My five years there were filled with success and real artistic growth. I discovered that I could do things I hadn't realized I was capable of. We were experimenting all the time, and I got the chance to work with some very talented people. Some of my first arrangements at Mercury were done by an unknown young fellow named Henry Mancini.

Once, when we managed to finish the *Swamp Girl* session an hour early, I went up to Carl and suggested off the cuff that we record *Music, Maestro, Please*, one of my favorite old standards. He agreed, and we decided to work up a staged introduction. I asked if anyone in the band could handle a French accent, and it turned out one of the guys was French. We started the record with Carl playing cocktail music, then I walked in and struck up a conversation with a maitre d', requesting a special table and a tall drink. Then I asked for special music, sang the song, and bid my maitre d' friend goodnight before leaving the "club." We fostered the impression that I'd walked out the door by pausing and then having the piano player come back in and play a few blues riffs. We were just fooling around, but it turned into one of the first pieces of production ever done on a pop record.

Now I was anxious to start out in a big way with Columbia, and I was certain that I had just the song that would do it for me.

* * * * * *

Mitch Miller was certain that he'd found the first number for the new label, too. My choice was the song I'd been sent while at Ciro's, which I'd been guarding like a mother hen since it became obvious I was going to leave Mercury. The song was *Jezebel*, written by Wayne Shanklin, and the demo record I heard by a kid named Fred Darien was so fantastic that I think if it had been played on the air he might have become a star off the strength of that one song alone. I'd been very impressed by the Latin and Spanish sounds I'd heard while on my honeymoon, and this song fit right in that groove, using flamenco rhythms to whip up an atmosphere of sexual frustration and hatred while a guy berated the woman who'd done him wrong.

Mitch's song was more tame. The melody had been written in Shanghai and was originally recorded by a Chinese girl singer named Hue Lee. It was called *Mei Kuei.*

The record caught on with British and American soldiers stationed in the East, and they brought it back home with them. In England a BBC disc jockey named Wilfred Thomas, who ran a popular program called *Record Rendezvous*, crafted some English lyrics for it about a soldier bidding farewell to his sweetheart and entitled the result *Rose, Rose, I Love You.*

When I got back to New York to open at the Copa, Mitch, Carl and I huddled to compare notes. I played him the demo of *Jezebel*, and he said, "Oh yeah, that's going to be a big one, but mine's every bit as good." I didn't agree. I was certain that the American public would find Spanish-sounding music more exciting, and I wasn't too sure they'd go for an Oriental song with that peculiar Eastern tonality.

March 30 was my 38th birthday, and the day after that my contract with Mercury officially expired. I was all set to go in and record the new material, but Mitch had a superstitious hang up about doing the songs on April Fool's Day. So we waited a day and released the two songs back to back on April 10. I've always been lucky with first releases, and this one turned out to be a two-sided hit for us with both songs going gold. This time I'd outguessed Mitch, though, because *Jezebel* turned out to be far the more popular and lasting song. I still close every show with it. It gets such a big reaction that we can't fit it anywhere else in the line-up except at the end. It was also our first record to become a big hit in Europe, and this lifted me to a heady state of international recognition.

* * * * * *

Towards the last half of 1951, all of the touring, recording, and overuse finally caught up with my overworked throat. It's almost inevitable that sometime while on the road you'll be exhausted, run into bad weather, and catch a miserable cold. Unfortunately, nobody is sympathetic. If you have a heart attack or break a leg people understand, but if you tell them you've caught a cold and can't sing, they look at you like you're trying to get away with something. They don't realize that there's nothing worse for a singer than to attempt to sing over a cold. You can try to fake a show by doing the easy things, but when they request the tough material and you give it your best shot, you're only compounding your throat problems.

Through overwork and oversinging you can also develop nodes or polyps (that happened to Bing Crosby early in his career). Sometimes the wound goes deeper and becomes like an open sore. That's referred to as contact ulcers, and that's what happened to me. They usually occur in the middle of your vocal chords, making it difficult for your middle and anterior parts to produce a sound. You end up forcing a sound by straining and using the back parts of your vocal chords that normally only come into play when you holler "Help!" or scream at a football game. Obviously this isn't a very good idea, but when you earn your livelihood with your throat, what can you do? My problem kept getting worse.

By the time December rolled around I was busy at Columbia making my third picture there, *Rainbow 'Round My Shoulder*. During the shooting, I started honking like that wild goose I was always singing about. I couldn't get a sound going until late in the day, after I'd had honey and lemon, tea, coffee, juice, and every other home remedy anybody could think of. Off the set, I couldn't even talk. To communicate at home, Nan and I exchanged little notes. After the picture was in the can the conductor (Morris Stoloff, who became one of my dearest friends) asked me about my problems. He recommended that I go see Dr. Barney Kully, a throat specialist in Beverly Hills who'd treated nearly all the big singers at one point in time.

I was leery, because I had already gone to four other doctors and been diagnosed four different ways. Two of them advised operating, two of them didn't. I went in to see Dr. Kully the first thing on Monday morning, and we'd barely shaken hands before he said, "Don't say anything, just let me examine you." After a complete examination he said, "Operating we can always do. Let's try everything else first. Now, I don't want you to talk until you come in to see me again tomorrow morning." The next day he told me the same thing and added that he went horseback riding on Wednesdays, so I'd have to stay quiet until Thursday. Using variations on this theme, he conned me into keeping my mouth shut for the next nine weeks.

After that my throat improved considerably, but I had another serious problem in the form of a tenuous piece of filament hanging down from my uvula, which feels like having a string dangling in the back of your throat. I'd never known it was there, except for the fact that I often felt like something was in my throat and used to "har-rumph" frequently to try and clear it. I later learned that this is a very bad habit that singers should avoid. Dr. Kully removed it and from then on I was fine, although I got a real scare right after he snipped it off when my throat reacted by swelling up and for a while it felt like I couldn't breath.

After he bailed me out, Dr. Kully sent me to a vocal coach named Lillian Goodman, just to see if I might have any problems with my breathing that I wasn't aware of. I visited her office and she said, "I don't know what you're doing wrong, but you sing great. Don't fool with your style. Let's just improve your breathing, if that's where the problem is." For three weeks she coached me on the proper techniques, and at the end of that time she'd increased my range by one note on the top and one on the bottom. After that, my throat troubles were over.

With my voice restored I felt ready to take on the world, which was a good thing, because that's just what I was about to do. My follow-up releases to *Jezebel* had done extremely well. Carl and I reworked the old standard, *Jealousy*, into a sort of jazz tango that shot into the top five and went gold in a matter of weeks. Terry Gilkyson came back after *Wild Goose* with a song called *The Girl in the Wood*. It was reminiscent of *Swamp Girl,* and though it didn't do well in the States it became a tremendous hit in England. Things had really broken wide open for us over there.

Wilfred Thomas, the BBC disc jockey who'd written lyrics for *Rose, Rose I Love You*, would play the song at least once per show. When the Brits bought my record, took it home, and listened to *Jezebel* on the other side, they went crazy.

It wasn't long before Milt Krasny, the man who had walked into Billy Berg's five years ago and arranged my Mercury recording contract, approached me with a marvelous suggestion.

"Frank," he said, "I think it's time for you to go to England."

Scene from *Sunny Side of the Street*, 1951.

With Bob Hope and Hedy Lamarr at a show we performed at the North Island Naval Air Station in San Diego, 1954.

NINE

ACROSS THE ATLANTIC

The popular music fans of the late forties and early fifties were a special breed. I was one of the last singers lucky enough to click with what were called the bobby-soxers, teenaged female admirers who went to extreme (but usually harmless) lengths to express their affection. Some of them decided that my voice was "hexy," which they claimed was an old Pennsylvania Dutch word meaning "sexy, as in he," and they petitioned publishing companies to include it in their dictionaries. Many called themselves "Lainettes" and wore hair ribbons, sweaters, and socks with my name on them. Some used purple polish to paint L-A-I-N-E on their fingernails. The bobby-soxers would come to the shows and squeal so loudly that I'm certain they couldn't even hear the music they were making such a fuss over.

Mind you, this fanatical type of devotion occasionally got out of hand. In 1949 I was opening at the Fairmont Hotel in San Francisco when I was awakened at 3:00 am by the sound of someone violently retching outside my door. A fifteen year old girl named Lillian from San Jose had apparently been so frustrated by her inability to meet me that she tried to kill herself by taking poison outside my hotel room. Fortunately, she didn't succeed.

It wasn't just the girls who got out of hand, either. At one of my first record signings in a Detroit department store, so many people were pressing to get close to the glass-walled booth where I was sitting that for a time there was a serious danger of someone being crushed to death. I'll never forget the look on some of those trapped faces. Adulation is a wonderful thing, but not when it gets out of hand.

The kids grouped themselves into fan clubs, and pretty soon I saw mine spread beyond the United States to faraway places like Malta, Cairo, Johannesburg and Iceland. Two clubs even popped up in Baghdad! This welcome development came about partly because Columbia was able to give my records international distribution, and partly because the series of movie musicals I'd made in Hollywood did good box office overseas. The films were strictly B movie quickies that were frequently block-booked on a double bill with the latest Rita Hayworth release. I'm not particularly proud of them, but at least they provided many people with their first opportunity to match a face with the voice they'd been hearing. One of them, *Bring Your Smile Along*, also gave Blake Edwards his first opportunity to direct a picture. The film *Sunny Side of the Street* did particularly well in Britain, and that coupled with the impact of *Jezebel* prompted Val Parnell, who managed the Palladium in London, to coax me overseas.

Nothing could have prepared me for the thrill and excitement of the next several weeks. It began when I got my first glimpse of England by air and started to take in the great sense of tradition and history which so fills that country. British entertainment mogul Lew Grade met us at the airport and whisked us off to a huge press reception at the Prince of Wales Theater to talk about our upcoming run at the Palladium and various provincial theaters on the Moss Empires circuit. None of us slept that night. Nan, Carl, Pa and I stayed up and talked while huge crowds gathered outside our hotel. Unfortunately, my mother didn't join us on this trip because she was extremely prone to motion sickness. Not even the prospect of seeing Italy again could persuade her to travel overseas.

The opening night at the Palladium, August 18, 1952, was absolutely incredible. I was told that we broke the attendance records that had been set by Judy Garland and Danny Kaye. Since all of us sold out the house for the length of our stay, I didn't understand how they figured I'd set a new record. The way it was explained to me was that the Palladium had a set number of standing room spaces, say 100, that went on sale the morning of the show. Among the three of us, the standing room spaces for my show had sold the *fastest*. It was the first time I'd ever heard of setting a record by beating somebody's timetable.

At one of the first shows, a lady from the audience scrambled over an apron that had been placed over the orchestra pit and clambered up on stage. She was coming towards me when the orchestra struck up *God Save the Queen* and she froze, out of habit, in mid-stride. She was a tiny, middle-aged woman and she stood there on that stage shaking like a little robin. The look of sheer terror on her face was something to behold. I guess she was caught up in the crowd's enthusiasm, but it was obvious now that she was shocked by what she'd done.

Out of the corner of my mouth I whispered, "Don't panic!" We made a bizarre pair as we both stood stock still while they lowered the curtain. Once it was down, she looked at me and wailed, "Oh, I'm so mortified!," but I put an arm around her shoulder and told her not to worry. We went to my dressing room so she could relax and pull herself together. The management was all set to have the bobbies drag her away, but I wouldn't hear of it. To me she

Frankie and the bobby soxers.

With Marilyn Maxwell and Jerry Colonna.

Leaving for the first trip to England, 1952.

Outside the Palladium, London, 1952.

was symbolic of one of the warmest receptions I've ever experienced.

One night during the engagement, Mitch Miller gave me a transatlantic "big discovery" telephone call from New York. Before I left for England I'd gone out to the Coast to record a song from an upcoming Western movie. Mitch called to tell me that the film was out and it was a smash. He was certain it would garner an academy award or two, and he wanted me to include the theme song, *High Noon*, in my act right away. Carl improvised an arrangement from what he remembered of the record, and the next night we pulled out *Mule Train* and stuck in the new tune. The audience went crazy. I called Mitch back to tell him that we had a hit. He said, "I knew it. I only wish we'd got the soundtrack." No one had ever approached me about doing it (Tex Ritter did a marvelous job singing the song for the film). A nice consolation for having missed out on the soundtrack was the fact that my record went gold. A lot of people still expect to hear me when they catch *High Noon* on the late show.

After two **perfect** weeks at the Palladium, Nan and I went to Paris for the first time to rest before resuming the tour. The sightseeing and antique shops in London had been marvelous. Nan has an all-consuming passion for antiques that has crowded us out of living space more than once! The ambiance really brought out the tourist in us. Several times large crowds gathered at places we visited. Once or twice we needed a few bobbies to help us out of tight spots, but the attention was well meant and I relished it.

Jezebel had hit very big in France. Every time we visited a Parisian nightspot the house band launched into their own rendition. One evening Nan and I had dinner with Edith Piaf and her then fiancee Jacques Pills, whom we had met on our South American honeymoon. Piaf flipped over *Jezebel* and had Charles Aznavour, who was writing for her at the time, come up with a French lyric which they both later recorded. I don't know of any other covers that came out at the time.

It would take a lifetime to do Paris justice, but we only had a week. This meant that we ran around so much that the idea of resting fell by the wayside. There are so many treasures to enjoy. We'd met Jose Ferrer while in London, and we spent a fascinating afternoon at the Shepperton Studios watching him and John Huston filming *Moulin Rouge*. This gave us an interesting perspective on the works of Toulouse Lautrec which we saw while exploring the magnificent art in the Louvre and elsewhere.

In September we flew to Glasgow, Scotland, to open at the Empire Theater. We received another incredible reception. Local authorities asked us to arrive on Monday instead of Sunday to help with crowd control. I thought their fears were exaggerated until we landed and needed their help just to get out of the plane! A crowd of over 5,000 people gathered outside our hotel, and they wouldn't go away until I went out on a balcony and sang a few bars of *Rock of Gibraltar,* a song that had gone over very big in Britain. The police later asked me not to toss signed photos from my window, which I'd been doing at several stops, and to stop lingering at the stage door to greet fans. We were tying up traffic!

After a few more engagements in England I took my first trip to Italy, a very emotional experience. I'd heard tales of the land of my ancestors all my life, but before *Desire* hit I never thought I'd get the chance to see it. Italy is like a passionate woman with her arms flung wide open. Milan, Venice, Florence, and Rome. Each city we visited managed to top the one before it. A vocal coach once told me that I might have sung opera if I'd been trained for it, so I got a special kick out of Milan. There, at the home of La Scala, everybody was screaming for *Jezebel*.

I was especially moved by Sicily and the area around Palermo where my parents were born and raised. It was great to meet their former neighbors and dig into my past at the hall of records. Also, my father enjoyed a memorable moment in the limelight in Palermo. During a radio interview a reporter leaned over to Pa and said conspiratorially, "Tell me, can your son sing the old songs the way we used to do in the mountains long ago?" "No!" he replied, and then immediately broke it up by reliving the old days in song with a voice that sounded a lot like Jimmy Durante's. Pa could be quite a ham. He sailed home ahead of us on a different boat, and within twenty-four hours everyone on board knew who he was. Within forty-eight hours, he was emceeing talent shows.

* * * * * *

Back in the States, Mitch was full of new ideas. He decided to try me on what turned out to be a very successful series of duets with other Columbia artists. I'd done a duet with Patti Page while at Mercury, but I never considered harmonizing to be one of my strong points. Before I left Columbia I sang with Jo Stafford, Doris Day, the Four Lads, Johnny Ray, child star Jimmy Boyd, and others.

On the solo front, Mitch brought me three tunes which we recorded on the same night, all of which did very well. One, in fact, is my personal favorite and has become my biggest seller through the years (over 10,000,000 copies so far). The first song was *Someday*, an old tune from the Victor Friml operetta *The Vagabond King*. The second was *Granada*, for which we used a semi-classical arrangement with some difficult sustained notes. It was quite a challenge for me. The third song was *I Believe*.

I first heard *I Believe* when Mitch came out to see me in California to tell me about another great discovery of his. He sang four bars and believe me, singing is not one of his many talents. It's a testament to the song that I could sense its worth in spite of that (how should I put this?) *unique* voice of his! The lyrics were a simple but moving declaration of faith, and seldom had words touched me so deeply. It was almost more of a prayer than a song. In my life I've often turned to Him for comfort and guidance. I feel He's always come through, so the song didn't only speak to me, it spoke for me.

Countless times over the years people have told me how much they love *I Believe*, and how its sentiment has helped them through trying periods (one musician told me it helped him kick a heroin habit). This universal appeal made it a worldwide hit. In Britain it stayed on the charts for thirty-six weeks and sat at number one for eighteen of them, both unbeaten achievements that still stand in the record books today. This happened in spite of the fact that the BBC wouldn't play it! The lyric does not contain the words "God" or "Lord," but because it has such strong religious connotations they shied away from it. Such was their outlook at that time. Another song I recorded, *Answer Me, O Lord*, received almost no air play in the U.S. and abroad for the same reason. Nat Cole's version, which altered the lyrics to *Answer Me, My Love*, didn't have a problem.

Back in Hollywood, director Mervyn LeRoy noticed how well *High Noon* had done for me and asked me to perform *Blowing Wild* for a 1953 Warner Brothers production called *Black Gold*, starring Gary Cooper, Barbara Stanwyck, and Anthony Quinn. I was hesitant to do soundtrack work at first, because I figured that the picture itself was the most important thing and that a singer's contribution stood a good chance of being ignored or shunted off to the side. Instead, I found it was a great way to keep the voice in front of the public. I soon developed a reputation as a soundtrack singer. To date I've done the themes for seven movies and four television shows, mostly

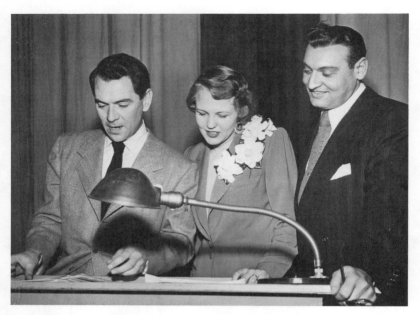

Getting ready for an appearance on **The Chesterfield Supper Club** with Peggy Lee and her husband, Dave Barbour.

Recording *Pretty Eyed Baby* with Jo Stafford.

westerns. After *Mule Train* and *High Noon*, every western song in creation was offered to me for consideration.

1953 also brought with it another tour abroad. The British fans had really taken our music to heart, so much so that in October of '53 three of the top four positions in their music chart were filled by my records. I went back to England and Scotland, and this time added Ireland to the itinerary. The receptions we got in Dublin and Belfast were as warm and raucous as those we received anywhere. There was also another visit to Vancouver. I don't think I've ever seen fans as enthusiastic as they were in Canada in those days. Back in 1948 at the Mutual Street Arena in Toronto, they had to dress me up as a cop and sandwich me in between several real policemen to get me safely out of the building. Talk about pandemonium!

It seemed like nothing could go wrong, as if I were being swept along with a tide I could no longer control, so I just sat back and enjoyed it. How could I suspect that in a few months my world would be shattered by a tragedy that would rob me in one blow of my best friend, my musical inspiration, and my desire to ever set foot on a stage again?

* * * * * *

In my diary, I marked down March 27, 1954, as the blackest day of my life. Since that time, the deaths of my mother and father have hit me harder, but not with the devastating suddenness that characterized the day Carl Fischer died.

My dear friend and accompanist had long suspected that he suffered from heart trouble, but two cardiographs had revealed nothing. He was scheduled to go in for a third on March 27. The night before he experienced intense pain and called a local drugstore at three in the morning, hoping to get some pills that would help. His left arm went numb, as it had done before, and he beat it with his right trying to get feeling. It hurt Carl to lie on his back, so his wife Terry rolled him over onto his stomach and after awhile she thought she heard him snoring before he dropped off to sleep. Sadly, she was probably listening to his last few gasping breaths.

It had been a rough night for Terry, too, and when she thought that Carl was finally resting she immediately fell asleep. When she awoke, one look told her that something was wrong. She felt for a pulse, then listened for a heartbeat, and was unable to get either. She called an ambulance, the police, and her doctor, but there was nothing anyone could do. Carl had been gone for hours.

Nan was given the horrible news first, and reached me by phone at the Riviera Country Club in Los Angeles just as I'd finished golfing and was walking up to the clubhouse. She wouldn't tell me what was wrong over the phone, but I knew by the tone of her voice it was something terrible. I drove home as quickly as I could, and the closer I got the stronger I sensed that this news concerned Carl. For some time I'd had a vague, uneasy feeling that something bad was going to happen, but I wasn't prepared for anything like this. Carl was only 41 years old.

When Nan confirmed my worst fears I nearly went out of my mind. We raced over to the Fischer's home in Sherman Oaks and Nan put her arms around Terry while I rushed into the bedroom.

I felt Carl and he was very cold. He was still wearing his wristwatch on his left arm, so I tried to unbend his right one out from under his head to feel for a pulse. It was a futile gesture, because he was already very stiff. I dropped to the floor by his side and cried, begging him to come back to me. No one quite knew what to do, but everyone somehow managed to do the right thing except for me. I was inconsolable.

I cancelled all my upcoming concerts and for two weeks hardly spoke a word to anyone. For once, instead of accepting a setback, I tried desperately to convince myself that it hadn't happened. Carl was irreplaceable. His love for music was so strong, and his powers of concentration were amazing. He used to sit at home and compose unbothered while the vacum cleaner droned, his two little daughters tore around and hollered, and the telephone rang off the hook. Once in Vancouver, he went on blithely playing while a brawl broke out in the club and sent glass bottles whizzing past our heads. On the other hand, he could be so absentminded about other things as to come on stage with long strips of tissue paper dangling from spots where he'd cut himself while shaving. We'd been through so much together that I wasn't sure I could go on without him. I wasn't sure I wanted to try.

Eventually, Nan helped to convince me of what I knew in my heart, that Carl wouldn't want me to throw away all we'd achieved together. I hired Al Lerner, a freelance arranger and pianist who'd worked with Harry James and later accompanied Dick Haymes, and accepted a booking in Chicago. We opened, of all times, on the tenth anniversary of the day I first met Carl. I tried hard to be strong, but I just didn't have the emotional or vocal control to get through the entire evening. I dropped my last number, *I Believe*, because I knew I couldn't do it justice that night. When the curtain fell after *Jealousy*, I broke down and cried on stage.

It was a long time before I felt completely comfortable before the footlights again, secure in the knowledge that Carl was with me in spirit. I gained that peace of mind by helping him to posthumously achieve one of his lifelong ambitions.

Off and on for fifteen years before his death, Carl had worked on an orchestral suite he entitled *Reflections of an*

Indian Boy. It was an autobiography in music meant to reflect the thoughts and feelings of a Native American, Cherokee Indian lad. This was a difficult undertaking for a self-taught musician, and he divided the piece into nine themes: *Reflections, At the Pool, Maiden's Prayer, Loma, Wedding Feast, Lullaby, Big Brave's Song, Squaw's Lament,* and *War Dance.* I was constantly after him to get the thing done, and helped out by writing lyrics for several of the themes. We auditioned parts of the piece for Victor Young, a distinguished conductor who'd also composed great movie music for films like *The Quiet Man* and *Samson and Delilah.* In the month or so before tragedy struck, Carl seemed obsessed with finishing his composition. He handed me the music for *War Dance,* the final part, four days before he died.

When Victor Young called to express his condolences, he was curious about whatever became of Carl's suite. I thought it had died with him, but Victor had kept a tape of our audition performance. He asked me to bring over the *War Dance* music, and completely of his own volition he sat down and scored the entire suite. He arranged to premier it with the Cleveland Symphony Orchestra on August 5, 1954. Before Carl's suite Victor conducted a program of his own music, and afterwards I did a show. Both of us donated our services in memory of Carl. It was wonderful sitting with Terry and Carl's two daughters, Carol and Terry, as a seventy piece orchestra performed his music to an appreciative audience of ten thousand people. A recording of the suite was later released by Columbia, and subsequently re-released by several different labels.

Carl and I had always been partners who shared in everything, but that night the well-deserved standing ovation was all his.

The Fischers and the Laines: Carl and Terry with their daughters, Carol and Terry; and Nan and me with Jan and Pam.

* * * * * *

My last record with Carl Fischer was an 1890s-style boxing ballad entitled, ironically, *The Kid's Last Fight*. It had been another tremendous hit for me in England, as had *My Friend*, a religious number in the same vein as *I Believe* (Eddie Fischer, who was a hot property at the time, released his version of *My Friend* in the U.S. before I did, so mine didn't do too much at home). It seemed like 1954 would certainly bring with it another big British tour, but I didn't realize how big until I received a surprise phone call while lounging in a Turkish bath in Hollywood. We were scheduled to cap off my next visit with a Royal Command Performance before Queen Elizabeth II.

Just before we left for England, Nan and I were slightly shook up in a traffic accident in Chicago. Now that I think back, this might have been meant to brace me for what happened when we landed in London. As a publicity stunt, the *New Musical Express* magazine arranged for a fleet of

133

buses to bring in fans to the airport to greet my plane. I had a genius of a publicity agent over there named Suzanne Warner, and we'd tried something like this before in 1953 when she organized a "fan convention" at the Festival Gardens in Battersea Park. The incredible crowds which showed up were described by one paper as "only to be compared with Picadilly Circus on Coronation Night," but at least that time they stayed under control. At the airport, things were different.

We landed on a calm Friday evening, September 24, and it wasn't until I reached customs that I became dimly aware of a muffled chanting outside. The place was loaded with policemen, and it turned out that U.S. Secretary of State John Foster Dulles was flying home that night after conferring with Prime Minister Anthony Eden. I assumed the commotion had something to do with him. When I realized with a start that the people were chanting "We want Frankie!" I gratefully got ready to go out and shake a few hands. The airport officials were worried that the fans might get out of control, so they asked me not to come too close to them. Instead, I was supposed to stand outside the public enclosure where the "welcoming committee" was waiting and address them en masse with a hand mike. When we reached the platform the mike turned out to be broken, and I made a big mistake by stepping forward so that people could hear me.

Before I grasped what was happening, the barricades broke down and we were engulfed by hundreds and hundreds of screaming young ladies. I was uncontrollably pushed back and found myself entangled with journalists, bicycles, packing crates and everything else that got in the way. Lew Grade lost a shoe in the confusion, and I soon found my own wardrobe being divvied up for souvenirs. We ended up hiding behind a tool shed, seeking shelter from the fans. I'd been mobbed before, from Detroit to Glasgow, and as a rule I don't scare easily, but this time I

Signing autographs in the Festival Gardens in London, 1953.

was really worried. Someone could easily have broken a leg or worse in that throng. The police decided that the only way to restore order was for me to leave the airport, so they hustled me off the grounds. I really had no choice. The next day the headline read "HE CAME. HE SAW. HE BOLTED."

After a very exciting tour which included stops in Manchester, Leicester, Liverpool, Edinburgh and Dundee, I flew to Paris to meet Nan and play a date with the Vic Lewis Orchestra at the Alhambra. We returned to the London Palladium to perform for the Queen on November 1. *I Believe* had been the number one song in Britain during Coronation week, and I was thrilled with this opportunity. Every performer was restricted to two songs or less, and I chose *Jezebel* and *Sunny Side of the Street.* Afterwards, they chose twelve of us to go out into the foyer and meet the Queen as she went down a reception line and greeted everybody. This gave my p.r. lady another clever idea, and this time, everything worked out fine.

I had become good friends with Joe Carleton, the official photographer of this event, who worked with one alternate photographer. Together they took a picture of each person being introduced to the Queen. The picture that turned out most complimentary to the Queen was the one picked up by the wire services and run by newspapers all over the world in reporting the event. Joe told me that I should try and be tenth in line because, from previous experience, it was at that distance from the camera that the Queen always took her best picture.

With a little effort I managed to jockey myself into the right position, just between Bob Hope and Noel Coward. When we met, I could barely hear the Queen above all the commotion. She mentioned *Jezebel* (I assumed she liked it!), and we made some small talk about the sights I'd seen while touring. After we finished our brief conversation and she moved down the line, I looked across to Joe and he smiled and circled his fingers to tell me that he'd got it. In no time at all Phillips, Columbia's record distributor in Europe, got a copy of the picture and sent it to New York. There, somebody at Columbia Records grabbed a handful of songs and slapped them together into an album entitled *Command Performance* (what rationale they used for choosing the songs, I don't know. They included *Jezebel*, but that was only one of the two songs that I'd actually performed for the Queen). Of course, they put my picture with the Queen on the front, and I have to credit their ingenuity. It cost their promotion department absolutely nothing to get advance publicity for the cover of my next release. It was featured on the front page of major newspapers all over the world.

The Royal Command Performance proved to be, if you will forgive me, a crowning achievement. I felt I was at the top of my game a few days afterward when we took the boat train to Southhampton and boarded the *Ile de France* to sail home. This was in 1954. Little did I realize that I was returning to a country where a variety of forces were about to combine to turn the popular music scene upside down.

Meeting the Queen. The picture that later became the cover of the Columbia album, *Command Performance*.

Perry Como, Frankie Laine, and Frank Sinatra. Cover of May 1951 issue of **Metronome**

TEN

CHANGES

A long-term, gradual shift in taste dramatically affected popular music in the mid-fifties. Radio stations began featuring rhythm and blues tunes, usually performed by black artists, in their programming. In the early days those records were referred to as "race records" (a term I never cared for), implying that they had been recorded by blacks solely for an ethnic market. Now these sounds were being pushed into the mainstream by people like Alan Freed, a disc jockey out of Akron, Ohio. He wanted to spread his wings and become a promoter, so he started packaging rhythm and blues shows to compete with several that were already on the road. These revues consisted of a bunch of marvelous entertainers: dancers, rhythm singers, and an orchestra.

In 1954 Bill Haley came out with a song called *Rock Around the Clock* and soon found he had the biggest record in the country. Eventually all of these sounds, plus some music that was coming up from the rural South and New Orleans, were grouped together under the heading "Rock and Roll." It began to catch on in metropolitan areas and then all of a sudden, seemingly out of nowhere, came a kid named Elvis Presley with a song called *Heartbreak Hotel*.

I remember going to see Elvis at his first Las Vegas engagement at the New Frontier Hotel in 1956. He had been booked with a big band, and the Vegas crowd couldn't identify with what he had to offer. He didn't go over well at all. After the show his manager, Colonel Tom Parker, asked Nan and me to come over and join Elvis for a while at his table. He was a shy, likeable youngster who politely told me that he'd be happy to do half as well for himself as I'd done in my career. At the time, I don't think any of us realized that his style marked the dawn of a new era.

Mitch Miller absolutely hated rock and roll, and his resolve against it severely hampered his career as an A & R man. He refused to allow anyone that he had any control over to record rock, which was just as well, because none of the big names on Columbia's roster at the time were really suited for it (or cared for it!). It certainly wasn't in Tony Bennett's or Rosemary Clooney's ballpark. Jo Stafford had that pure, liquid-silver voice which wouldn't have worked. Johnny Ray might have been more readily accepted by the rockers if he hadn't become popular before the rock era, because he was doing similar things with music in the early fifties. Guy Mitchell sounded too country.

That left me. I was willing to experiment, but Mitch wouldn't go any further than trying to sneak in the back door with a couple of half-assed, semi-rock tunes called *Bubbles* and *You Know How It Is*. I think if we were going to mess with this new form, we should have gone all out with a real strong song. A rock and roll treatment of one of my old rhythm tunes, *Ain't That Just Like a Woman*, for example, which was essentially a boogie blues, might have shown some people how much rock owed to a lot of what had come before. Instead of leaping in, we stuck a toe in the water and decided we didn't want to swim. My "rock inspired" recordings were lousy.

* * * * * *

In spite of rock's takeover, the mid-fifties were still an exciting time for me on wax. The long playing album was a new development, and in 1955 I recorded the first two twelve-inch albums on Columbia Records. The first was a record I made with the Four Lads called *Spirituals,* a pop-oriented gospel collection which yielded a successful single in *Rain, Rain, Rain.*

The second was a special treat, a real career highlight that many fans have told me they consider my best work. It was called *Jazz Spectacular,* and I recorded it in October of 1955 between shows at the Latin Quarter in New York. I usually don't like to record while playing clubs, because all that continuous singing gives my voice a harsh edge that only goes away after it's been rested. This session was so full of good feelings and mutual admiration that it proved a welcome exception to the rule. I had the privilege of working with Buck Clayton and his Orchestra, an all-star crew that included J. J. Johnson and Kai Winding on trombone (they had a great "battle" with each other on *Taking a Chance On Love*). We did wonderful old standards like *S'posin'* and *Stars Fell on Alabama,* and every session was like a trip in a time machine back to good old Billy Berg's.

In 1955 and 1956 I had my first glimpses of Australia and New Zealand. The fans in Sidney, Melbourne, Brisbane, Auckland, and Wellington were as enthusiastic and kind as they had been in Europe. Back in the States, my agency decided that television might be a good way to keep in front of the public while the music charts reflected the changing times.

I'd filmed a series of fifteen-minute television shows for Guild Films in London in the early fifties, but this time we broadcast live for CBS. The show was fairly successful, but aside from some enjoyable guest appearances over the years I've never felt totally at home on television. For one thing, I don't like to wear my glasses when I work, but on T.V. I had to be able to find my marks and read the cue cards (not to mention avoiding the edge of the orchestra pit!). Also, a broadcast every week put you in danger of overexposure. No medium devours material like television. Back in those days there was the added bother of commuting from Los Angeles to New York, with the need to maintain two households and all the hassle that entails. Last but not least, the shows went out live, and all the rehearsal in the world didn't guarantee a thing once you got on the air. (At one of our rehearsals Jackie Gleason dropped in, uninvited and unannounced, by driving a big pink Cadillac full of showgirls onto the center of our soundstage. He hopped out, said, "Just thought I'd drop in and see how things are coming along!" and proceeded to make a shambles of the set, breaking up the cast and crew for the rest of the afternoon.)

I'd long had good reason to be wary of live television, dating back to 1953 and the time I sang *I Believe* on *The Ed Sullivan Show*.

I had introduced a lot of songs on Ed's stage, and I always enjoyed the way the music was showcased. To set the mood for *I Believe*, they decided to dress me up as a small town preacher and have me drive a horse and buggy into the middle of a gathering of "townsfolk," where I was supposed to sing the song as if delivering a sermon. The horse must have misunderstood the title to be *I Relieve*, because I was barely four bars into the tune when he started to make a complete mess of the stage. Marlo Lewis, the producer of the Sullivan show, later wrote that in the control room they heard the cameraman exclaim, "Holy Mother! That horse has some piss power!" into his intercom.

The nag took thirty-two seconds to empty his bladder, and he wasn't finished yet. As the horse proceeded to make things even messier, they signaled me that it was time to step down off the buggy into the middle of the "congregation." Fat chance. I somehow managed to finish the song and drive the buggy off-stage. The studio audience was hysterical, and the acrobatic dance team which followed me on had one hell of a rough night.

Even if it's not my favorite medium, I can't deny that television has always had a tremendous power to communicate. It was brought home to me the night I appeared on *This Is Your Life*. The show was broadcast on the evening of our wedding anniversary. I thought I was looking forward to a night out on the town. Instead, I ended up in a big television studio with Ralph Edwards and my family all around me for a sentimental journey through the past. After the show, Martha Raye called me long distance from across the country. Now, I hardly knew Martha well enough to say "Hello," but she loved the idea of family. She had been deeply moved by the sight of the whole big, happy LoVecchio clan together on the screen, and she called just to share her feelings.

I was pretty touched myself.

* * * * * *

In 1955 I made my last film at Columbia, *He Laughed Last,* and this one at least had something resembling a plot and gave me the chance to do a little acting. This led to a few more dramatic guest shots on television shows like *Perry Mason*, which I really enjoyed. If I have one major career regret, it's that I never had the opportunity to go further in this field. Most of my time at the movie studios was spent singing, on and off screen. In 1955 I went to Universal to record the title track for *The Man Without a Star*, then it was over to Warners for *Strange Lady in Town*. In 1956 I did *Gunfight at the O.K. Corral* at Paramount and

3:10 To Yuma at Columbia. This jazz singer was finding himself more and more identified with Western music.

In the middle of all this, and fighting uphill all the way against the onslaught of rock and roll, Mitch Miller managed to being me another million seller with *Moonlight Gambler* (the clip-clop sounds at the beginning of the record were actually made by Mitch clicking his tongue against his teeth). I thought it was a pretty good song, but it didn't have gold record written all over it the way that *Jezebel* did, so Mitch (who had a lot of confidence in it) and I made a bet. If it didn't sell a million he'd have to shave off his trademark beard, but if it did I had to grow one myself and keep it for at least six months. Thankfully I lost, so I grew a beard for the first time. I toyed with it on and off for a while after that, and now I sport whiskers regularly. Nan says my beard scratches, but otherwise there've been no complaints and I think it's here to stay.

Moonlight Gambler was yet another song with a western feel to it, and its success coupled with the movie soundtracks prompted a producer named Bill Dozier to approach me with an idea for a television series he'd been working on. Westerns were all the rage on T.V. in those days, and he'd decided to produce a show about the adventures of a group of men on a cattle drive and cast it completely with unknown actors. A lot of people in Hollywood thought he was crazy, but he was counting on the popularity of the genre to sustain the show until it became established. For added insurance, he decided it would be a big plus if he could get a name vocalist to do a song written specifically for the series.

Bill went to Dmitri Tiomkin and Ned Washington (the team responsible for *High Noon*) and told them he needed a song and it had to be called *Rawhide*. In three weeks they brought him their results and he called me in to the studio to hear it. I knew I was in for a sales pitch, but I didn't play it cagey or standoffish. I told him that I'd do it if the deal was right and I liked the music, and asked if I could see what would be happening on the screen while the song was being played. They screened an episode for me that wasn't all that memorable, but the opening scene really grabbed me. All of a sudden there were these guys hollering "Hyah! Hyah!" and riding into the picture with thousands of stampeding steers. The excitement was electric, and I told him I'd do it after just seeing that. It was one of the best moves I ever made, because it became another gold record and kept my voice on the air continuously from 1959 to 1966 (and in syndication ever since then).

It almost never happened. Part of the deal was that the record had to be released eight weeks before the show hit the air, which they'd hoped to do in September of 1958. The problem was that no one would sponsor an unknown cast (which included a young Clint Eastwood), and to go on the air without a sponsor is death unless you have a guaranteed hit show. The record was released on schedule, but the producers decided to delay airing the show until they were sponsored, which put the song in danger of dying on the vine.

Bill called and tried to placate me, pointing out that we'd invested about five thousand dollars in a song while he'd poured over two million into the series. He promised that they'd re-release the record as a promotional adjunct when the show finally hit the air. I thought that was fair enough, but Mitch Miller was furious. "Who the hell do those blankety-blanks think they are?" was his reaction. He'd foreseen the possibility that I might have another record going places that could be short-circuited by a re-release of *Rawhide*.

They finally got their sponsors and hit the air in January of 1959. Sure enough, I had another record getting a little attention at the time, a song called *When I Speak Your Name*. Who knew that *Rawhide* would soon become one of the top rated shows in the country? The first record just petered out, while *Rawhide* became a smash the second time out. For the first four months, the theme song kept that show on the air. Clint Eastwood later told me that people had told him they turned the show on to hear the song, turned it off and waited an hour, and then turned it on again to hear it over the closing credits.

When I came onto the set to do a guest shot in 1960, Eric Fleming, Clint, and the rest of the cast all shook my hand and thanked me for keeping them in business. The guest appearance was especially memorable for me, because it brought Nan out of hiding (she'd quit movies shortly before we were married, and never really enjoyed the life of a contract player). *Rawhide*'s producer, Charles Marquis Warren, was one of Nan's big fans from her movie days, so he coaxed her into playing a sheriff's wife and there we were, doing a love scene opposite each other. It was a special moment for both of us, and a dream come true for me.

Rawhide was my last professional association with Mitch Miller, bringing to an end what was, after Carl, the second most rewarding musical partnership of my career. We explored so much new territory, and I can only remember two real mistakes made during our time together. On the heels of *Jezebel* somebody other than Mitch brought me *Witchcraft*, which we turned down because I thought its theme was too similar and its music less exciting. Then Mitch brought me a really crazy record with lyrics I didn't understand at all. After I turned it down, he took *Come On A My House* over to Rosemary Clooney to see if she might be interested.

Towards the late fifties Mitch grew tired of bucking the trend in popular music and began searching for a new direction. He came up with his *Sing Along With Mitch* program, on television and on records, and became a national celebrity in his own right. He felt a little guilty, though, about leaving all his Columbia artists in the lurch.

Only two of the old guard, Tony Bennett and I, emerged relatively unscathed. Both of us owe a great deal of the success we achieved at Columbia to the talents of Mitch Miller.

Today Mitch is happily back in his original element, visiting and conducting symphonies all over the country.

* * * * * *

Aside from the musical happenings in 1955, 1956, and 1957, I was also privileged during those years to play a part in one of the greatest "triple plays" in the history of sports. The game was golf, not baseball, and at the beginning I had no idea what I was getting myself into.

In 1955 I was invited by Wilbur Clark to participate in the festivities surrounding his Desert Inn's Las Vegas Tournament of Champions. Every year the Desert Inn Country Club's 7102 yards, par 36-36-72 course played host to a group of the greatest golfers in the country as they battled for a share of $40,000 (first prize was represented by a pile of 10,000 silver dollars sitting by the last hole. These amounts seemed spectacular at the time, but look like peanuts now compared to what golfers earn today). This event had been nicknamed "The Slot Machine Open" because of the annual betting auction, called a Calcutta, which preceded it.

Celebrities auctioned off the various golfers to the highest bidder and the total amount bid was pooled, less twenty percent which was donated to the Damon Runyon Cancer Fund. If you bought the right guy, you stood to make an extremely healthy profit. I had been asked to serve as one of the auctioneers.

On the long drive to Las Vegas Nan suggested that it might be a nice gesture on my part to bid on one of the golfers, since I frequently performed at the Inn's Painted Desert Room. She'd seen a picture of one of them in the paper, a 24 year old lad from San Diego named Gene

Littler, and she liked the way he gripped his club. I decided she had a point and made a mental note of the name.

When we got to the auction I was a little nervous, having never experienced one before. Bob Hope, Danny Kaye, Walter Winchell, and others were on hand for the same reason I was, and when I asked what I should do, they told me to just relax and watch Hope, then do what he did. Before the bidding started I discussed the possibility of going in together on a bid with Jack Rael, Patti Page's manager. We decided to try it and agreed not to go over three thousand dollars for our guy.

After a big dinner, the golfers left the room and the auction started. When I saw that the opening bid was eight grand for somebody named Peter Cooper, who was not exactly a favorite, I got Jack's attention (he was sitting across the room from me) and waved goodbye. This thing was looking to be too rich for my blood. Having been thoroughly acquainted with all aspects of poverty, I was never a rash man with a dollar. Before the evening was over, favorites like Carey Middlecoff and Sam Snead went for sixteen and seventeen thousand dollars each. I managed to get through my stint as auctioneer, selling Julius Boros for $8,000, and was prepared to sit back and just watch when I noticed something very interesting.

Bob Hope made a substantial winning bid on Middlecoff and, after he got him, he was surrounded by newspaper men and popping flashbulbs. They took pictures of Bob smiling and pointing to his bid, which was written out on a large chalkboard on the wall. It occurred to me that he'd already earned back the price of his bid in free publicity. I sensed a marvelous opportunity here to pull another *Command Performance*-like stunt.

When the bidding got around to Littler, I opened with $10,500. When someone else went higher I did too, and I finally got my pick for $13,000. A lot of my friends were surprised, and after the hysteria of the moment had passed, I too had to wonder at what I'd got myself into. Gene was an 8-1 long shot.

To everybody's astonishment he didn't just win, he absolutely **dominated** a tournament in which 15 to 25 mile an hour winds and rain ruined most of the other golfer's games. The year before, Gene's first year as a pro, he'd come in seventh. This time his margin of victory was thirteen strokes. Nothing like that had happened since Ben Hogan won the '45 Portland Open by fourteen strokes, and that triumph had been against a much lesser field. Our little wager netted us a return of $72,000.

The next year, 1956, we were determined to buy Gene again even though the chances of a repeat were unlikely. This time we had to cough up $16,500 to land him. As a gesture of support, I spent the entire tournament standing in the gallery wearing a pair of bright, fire engine-red pants so Gene wouldn't have any trouble spotting me. I was rewarded for my troubles by watching Gene, with icy resolve and his machine-like swing, cruise to an easy four stroke victory. This time his win brought us $69,000. After he sank a tricky putt on the eighth hole, one of the bystanders turned to another and said, "You just can't beat the three L's."

"What're they?" his friend replied.

"Littler, Laine, and the Lord."

In 1957 there was very little doubt about where my money was going, but most people thought yet another bet on Littler was just money down the drain. Gene was in terrible form, and hadn't even won bus fare since the 1956 Calcutta. He went off at 12-1. Nan and I bought space in the Tournament's program and ran the following message:

Personal to Gene Littler—

We'll be looking forward to meeting you at the pile of 10,000 silver dollars at the end of the tournament, just as we did in 1955, 1956.

Nan and Frankie Laine

We kept that date.

In 1958, Gene tied for fourth and earned back the cost of our bid. In 1959 I had to come up with $26,000 to get him, the most that had ever been bid for a golfer in a Calcutta. He came in third and we doubled our money. some columnists began to wonder if Gene claimed me as a dependent on his income tax, and one figured out that our total earnings for the first three tournaments worked out to $5,325 per hour for four days work a year. Nan and I took our share and added the "Gene Littler Room" to our house in Beverly Hills, with a plaque over the door and memorabilia like tees, balls, replica checks, and Gene's cap on the walls. Gene's streak also piqued my interest in my own game, and golf became a consuming passion until I replaced it with sportfishing in the '60s.

Our "partnership" ended after 1959 when the PGA became wary of Calcuttas and, worried that gambling might have a bad influence on the play, brought these events to an end. That doesn't take away in the slightest, however, from one of the great feats in sports history.

* * * * * *

1956 brought with it the beginning of one of the most rewarding artistic collaborations of my career. While in New York on business I attended a cocktail party that was thrown at the Park-Sheraton to introduce a studious looking newcomer from France named Michel Legrand to the American public. He'd just recorded his first album of instrumental music, *I Love Paris*, and everyone at the party received a complimentary copy of his follow-up release, *Castles in Spain*.

When I arrived I immediately headed over to a group of familiar faces, Mitch Miller and some fellow Columbia executives. Standing with them was a tall, lanky, stern-faced young guy wearing rimless glasses that reminded me of a schoolmaster. One of the executives, George Avakian, spoke French, so he introduced me to the bespectacled fellow who turned out to be the guest of honor. I gathered he was a Frankie Laine fan, because when he realized who I was he threw his arms around me, kissed me on both cheeks, and shouted *"Formidable! Formidable!"*

Later that night when I went home and listened to his album, I gave out with a few superlatives myself.

Spanish music has always been a favorite of mine, and I thought *Castles in Spain* was brilliant. I knew right away that I had to record with this guy, and I could hardly wait to call Columbia the next morning and start the wheels in motion. Irv Townsend, who had stepped in as my producer after Mitch Miller, called Paris and put the idea to Michel. He was all for it, but it took us a year to coordinate our schedules. We decided to record in Paris, which meant a nice vacation for Nan and me. This project kept looking better all the time.

We arrived to find that somebody had been misinformed and Michel was on tour in Russia. He would be gone for the entire two weeks we were supposed to have spent working on the arrangements together. That really hurt, because this album was a difficult and demanding project. We'd decided to make it an international collection with songs sung in English, Spanish, French, Italian, and Portuguese. To keep the two weeks from being a total loss, we hired a linguist to coach me on the French and Spanish. The Italian came to me easily and the Portuguese I worked out phonetically. The song in English was an update of my old Mercury recording, *Mam'selle*.

When Michel got back to Paris he found that all his copies of the music had been lost. You've got to try and make the best of a bad situation, and I've never been one to make waves, but our starting date kept being pushed back until it coincided with a two week run my agent had booked at the Olympia Theater in Paris. This bothered me because, as I mentioned earlier, I don't like the way I sound when I work nights and then record during the day. Now it couldn't be avoided.

In the studio I was confronted with fifty musicians and an engineer named Pierre who wasn't familiar with my singing style. This scared the hell out of me. I knew that now, on top of everything else, there was little likelihood of getting the sound balances right. I came up with the idea of Michel just recording the music and then giving me the dubs so my voice could be overdubbed back in the States. I'd done this before with *Wild Goose*, but this was going to be much tougher because of the strange languages and intricate arrangements. Michel understood what I wanted and did a beautiful job of putting the whole thing together, recording his music while I sang the lyrics softly into his ear so the microphone wouldn't pick them up.

After we finished I flew home and waited for the results. The trip overseas, by the way, hadn't been a total loss. While at the Olympia I had the chance to renew my acquaintance with Edith Piaf and Charles Aznavour. Piaf invited Nan and me to a big party she threw at her estate in Richebourg, and Aznavour and I spent a pleasant evening playing troubadour, singing and strolling though the courtyards of Paris.

Two months later I got the music and made some copies that I could listen to while I overdubbed. I re-recorded my part onto another set of records and when it was all over I knew I could do better (you almost always think you can after a playback). I spent a month wearing the hell out of those records through repeated listenings and then went back into the studio and did it again. Nan suggested the title *Foreign Affair*. The album was soon released to sparkling reviews and miserable sales figures. We'd outsmarted ourselves.

The French didn't give a damn about what I sang in Italian, Spanish, or Portuguese. The Portuguese couldn't have cared less for French or Italian songs. English speaking people as a rule don't care for songs in foreign languages. I was stuck with a record that nobody was buying, even though it was critically acclaimed as a masterpiece. It looked like time to write the whole thing off to experience when some genius at Columbia came up with an inspired idea. He made a single out of *La Paloma* in Spanish and *Nao tem solucao* in Portuguese and released it in Brazil and Argentina. *La Paloma* was the A-side and a hit in Argentina, and *Nao tem solucao* sold like wildfire in Brazil. This success bailed out the project and helped to smooth the way for another, more conventional collaboration.

We made arrangements for Michel, who'd been married in the meantime, to come and stay at our house for a whole month while we picked songs and worked on the music together. Our daughter Pam generously moved out of her bedroom and in with Jan. We were all thrilled to have this great musician staying with us. He would sit in our living room and play for hours. I have some improvisations on tape you'd have to hear to believe.

One of the songs we selected was *Blue Moon*, my special song with Nan. Nan warned Michel, only half-jokingly, that she'd emasculate him if he didn't write the arrangement she knew he was capable of. When Michel sits down to write he can get obsessed with what he's doing. I've seen him stay at it for ten hours without interruption, and sometimes it's hard to read what he scribbles down in his hurry. I'll never forget the night he started working with

153

Blue Moon. We came home from a party, and he sat down at midnight and didn't budge until the arrangement was finished at ten the next morning. Two copyists came in. One guy had to relieve the other around six in the morning. They worked swing shifts, for Christ's sake! And that arrangement is a classic. There is an eight bar duet between the first trumpet and trombone that was a hot topic of conversation among studio musicians in Hollywood for quite some time.

I learned during this time that Michel was a big fan of Stan Kenton's and that he'd studied many arrangements of songs like *Tampico* that Stan had mailed to him after he was through with them. In that way Michel learned a lot of progressive, contemporary techniques that put him far out in front of the average arranger. While we were working on the album entitled *Reunion in Rhythm*, I threw a big party at my house and invited Stan and a lot of other people to hear what we were doing. Michel became the talk of Hollywood and people began dropping by the recording studio out of curiosity.

One of them was my young friend and "discovery," Andre Previn. He sat in on piano one night and we had a very special jam session where we recorded *I'm Confessin'* and a few other classics. Those were exciting nights, and I'm still stunned at what Michel was capable of bringing out in me. Many people have told me they feel that the quality and impact of those records remain undiminished, even after thirty years. He had a great influence on my life, and I like to feel I had a great influence on his. We started introducing him to some movie people and it wasn't long before he was assigned his first film score and began developing into the international superstar he is today.

I'd never spent much time worrying, but after my work with Michel was followed by the huge success of *Rawhide*, it was reassuring to know that the shifting musical scene still held a place in the shade for a lucky old son like me.

ELEVEN

NOT THROUGH YET!

After his help in arranging my collaboration with Michel Legrand, I felt secure that Irv Townsend could successfully fill Mitch Miller's shoes as my new producer at Columbia. He was a brilliant guy who'd been a clarinet player in his younger days before he was afflicted by palsy. His style as a producer was very different from Mitch's. Rather than constantly suggest material, he went along with whatever the artist wanted to do. He felt that performers were more inclined to give their best when involved with a pet project.

It seemed to me that the natural way to follow up the success of the *Rawhide* single was to release an entire album of Western songs and call it *Rawhide*, too. We used the movie soundtracks I'd made, and enough time had passed so that I was able to re-record some things I'd done at Mercury, like *Mule Train* and *Wild Goose*. There were legal complications that prevented us from calling the album *Rawhide*, so in 1961 we released it instead as *Hell Bent For Leather*. The record took off like a shot and stayed on the charts for a long time.

In the meantime, I acquired a wonderful new musical partner. In 1960 I went to New York to play the Waldorf-Astoria for the first time, with a drummer named Stanley Kay and guitarist Joe Sinacore. Al Lerner had left us to go back and work in Hollywood, so Joe was handling the music. I was searching all over for a new piano player when Stan reminded me about Ray Barr, who'd worked with Patti Page and Martha Raye for many years. We'd used him before, as a pick-up pianist for a 1960 South American tour, and he'd done fantastically well. Ray was a solid, stable family man around my age, which was a good thing. The other guys were family men, too. I've never liked working with wild musicians.

When I approached him he was busy doing rehearsals with Mary Martin for *Peter Pan*, but he agreed to double for us at night. Ray and I became good friends during this engagement. In many ways he reminded me a lot of Carl. They were both writing all the time. A lot of guys never sit down to work on or suggest new arrangements unless you make a direct request. Ray also watched his music case like a hawk. (This was very much like Carl. Once, after a benefit concert when for a moment it seemed as if our music had been lost in the shuffle, I watched the blood drain from Carl's dark, handsome face as it slowly turned chalk white.) After a 1962 engagement at the San Juan Intercontinental in Puerto Rico, Joe Sinacore's wife became sick and he also left us. Ray took over as my full-time arranger, conductor, and accompanist, and it stayed that way, very happily, for the next 21 years.

I convinced Irv Townsend to move out to California to handle Columbia's West Coast Office. He'd never liked New York, and having him close at hand would make coordinating our projects that much easier. When Ray Barr also came out West we were ready to begin work on my next record. I'd come up with the idea of a gambling album as a belated follow-up to *Moonlight Gambler*. We called it *Deuces Wild* and did songs like *Luck Be A Lady* from *Guys and Dolls* and *The Man Who Broke the Bank at Monte Carlo*. Unfortunately, we were now approaching the end of my contract with Columbia and they were reluctant to put out the money for the promotion the new record needed. I felt they let me down, especially after the big success of *Hell Bent for Leather*. After a few more projects, the label and I parted ways.

When my contract was up in 1963, I expected there to be the usual haggling. What I didn't expect was that the breakdown in negotiations would coincide with an event that rocked the world. I went to New York in November to meet with Columbia executives in a suite at the St. Moritz hotel. I had arranged to have dinner with a friend that evening, and just before the contract meeting started he called with the news that President Kennedy had been assassinated in Dallas. Stunned, I put down the phone and told the assembled group, "The President has been shot." For a while we just sat in silence and traded incredulous looks. Then, without a word spoken, everyone bolted from the room. At a terrible moment like this, our place was at home with our loved ones.

After the meeting broke up that way, I knew that a change was forthcoming. With a tragedy like that on the nation's mind, nobody cared about renewing a recording contract for a singer who'd already been with the label 14 years. I sensed deep inside that our negotiations would never be resumed. And they never were.

I fulfilled my commitment to Columbia by cutting two more albums and a single. The first album was *Call of the Wild*, a bunch of outdoor, he-man sort of material that was cleverly arranged by John Williams in the days before his hugely successful film scores and his current job with the Boston Pops. After that we did *Wanderlust*, which gave me the chance to record one of my favorite songs, *Ghost Riders in the Sky*. People still holler their requests for that one today (though I always remind them that Vaughn Monroe had the hit record). One of the singles off that album, *Glory Road*, had a five minute vocal that scared away all the radio stations. This was before *MacArthur Park*, and the disc jockeys were reluctant to touch anything over three minutes.

I was at the point in my career where the hysteria surrounding most new pop idols had long since subsided. In a way it's better to get past that stage and earn what recognition you receive by the quality of your work, but it had been a while since my last real commercial single and I'd already stayed with Columbia twice as long as I had with Mercury. It was time to move on, but before I left I did take one more shot at a single. Columbia knew this was the end of the line, however, so they didn't do a damn thing about it.

I got together with Terry Melcher, Doris Day's son, who was trying to become a record producer in the contemporary rock vein. When he was younger he used to come over to my house and hang around with my daughter Jan. His favorite song was *I Believe*, so I knew the kid liked me. We picked a tune called *Don't Make My Baby Blue* and used the Nashville piano style that was so prevalent at the time, with a countrified guitar in the background. It almost caught on, and had I not been leaving Columbia I think they would have done much more to help it. It didn't go anywhere at home and only enjoyed a blip of popularity in England before dropping from sight.

That was the end of my stay at Columbia, closing the book on probably the most exciting and rewarding part of my career. While there I had the chance to work with some of the greatest talents in the business: Paul Weston, Percy Faith, Billy May, Frank Comstock, Frank DeVol, and others. I couldn't help but be proud of so many of the things I'd recorded for the label, and of the experiments we tried that built on and even surpassed some of the reaches we'd made at Mercury. An album of folk songs and slave laments called *Balladeer*, which I made in 1959 backed by a twelve-voice choral group, is a good example of how we stretched the boundaries that confined most pop singers of the era.

Columbia had two marvelous recording studios in New York. The one we called the 30th Street Studio was actually an old converted church in an Italian part of town. When the session was going to be a long one and we needed lots of energy, Mitch used to take us to a nearby Mom and Pop grocery store for mind-boggling sandwiches that were thicker than the Manhattan phone book. The other place was Leiderkranz Hall up on 58th Street, which had incredible natural acoustics. In case I ever needed to be brought back down to earth, the Hall was right across the street from WINS, where I'd sung for five bucks a week while trying to keep from starving to death.

Thank God, I didn't have to worry about where my next meal was coming from anymore. Instead, it was time to give serious thought to where my next record was coming from.

* * * * * *

After casting around, I reached an agreement with Capitol Records in June of 1964. I couldn't have picked a worse time to start with them. The Beatles were coming into their own, and Capitol was too preoccupied with them to give anyone new to the label much attention. In my two years there I recorded 25 sides, they released 19, and nothing happened with any of them. I started working with Nat Cole's former producer, Lee Gillette. We made an album of religious material called *I Believe*, and after that didn't sell I tried again with a young producer named Dave Axelrod. I've got a story for you about his taste in music that'll curl your hair! To this day, his judgment represents my biggest professional sorrow.

159

One afternoon I got a phone call from a friend of mine named Doug Lawrence, who was producing pictures out at MGM. He said an acquaintance, Dan Merrin, had just called him from New York to ask if he knew Frankie Laine. There was a song coming out of a Broadway show that he felt would be just right for me. Actually, he was certain it would make a great record no matter who recorded it.

When Dan brought a tape over to my house and played the song for me, I was just stunned. Here was another *I Believe*, another *Jezebel*, a song with "smash hit" written all over it. In a rush of excitement I got a hold of Ray Barr and we went up to see Dave Axelrod.

Now, I was still walking on eggshells at Capitol and no one had managed to pick a hit yet. Dave had been combing through material. He was a real hyper guy, always smoking and jumping up and down. He'd been a piano player until an accident damaged his left hand and he turned to producing. In his jittery way he sat and listened to the song, then said, "Yeah Frank, it's a lovely tune, but it's nothing compared to some of the stuff that I have waiting for you to look at and listen to."

I couldn't believe it. All I could say was, "Really?" I wasn't in any position to make waves, so I had to tell Dan Merrin that my producer had said "no." Reluctantly, he took back his copy of *The Impossible Dream*. Of course, it did great things for Jack Jones and several others. I just know it could have been one of the biggest records I ever had. Instead, I was forced to settle for some incredibly weak material like *Heartaches Can Be Fun* and some of the other "classics" from the files of Dave Axelrod.

Nothing good had happened by June of 1966, and I realized that there was no point in renewing with Capitol while the Beatles were ruling the roost. We shook hands and once again it was time for me to look elsewhere.

* * * * * *

This period was discouraging for me on records, but my concert tours started extending farther than ever. In 1964 I visited the Orient for the first time and played dates in Japan, Hong Kong, Taiwan, and Taipei. They were very successful, as was my first trip to South Africa a few years later. I managed to get back to Australia and also visited Canada again, where a one-nighter at a Vancouver club called the Cave provided me with one of my most treasured show business memories.

Louis Armstrong was in town the same night, and he finished before our second show so he came in to catch the act. When somebody passed the word to me backstage that Louis was in the audience, I began to shake a little. He'd been my idol for such a long time. It was a strange feeling to think that the man I couldn't hear enough of since the late 1920s was actually coming in to listen to *me*.

On stage with Louis Armstrong at the Cave Club in Vancouver, B.C., 1968.

Halfway through the set I paused to introduce him to the audience. He stood up, took a quick bow, and started toward the stage. Before I knew it, he was standing right there beside me. We started kidding and throwing ad-libs back and forth. I didn't dare ask him to perform, but if he volunteered his services I wasn't about to say no. To my delight, he offered to sing and then stepped up to the microphone to do *That's My Desire*. He had covered the record back in '47. I started to join him at the bridge, thinking that we would divvy the song up between us, but he playfully pushed me away. In that inimitable Armstrong rasp he growled, "This is my song!" He finished to a tremendous ovation, and I will always fondly remember the warmth that simply radiated from the man that night.

Louis managed to project happiness and optimism constantly, even though he faced heart-breaking discrimination throughout most of his career. In Las Vegas during the racially charged mid-60s, I had another, less pleasant encounter with a fellow entertainer. He took something I said the wrong way, and it ended up derailing an old friendship. It was a truly unfortunate misunderstanding that just got out of hand.

I was singing at the Dunes and Sammy Davis, Jr. came in to catch the late show. When I performed *Mule Train* in a showroom, I usually divided up the audience and had a contest to see which side of the room could shout loudest at certain points in the song. If there was a celebrity or a friend at the show, I asked that person to "head the mule train" and get the shouts going. I knew Sammy was coming into the show that night, so I picked him.

At this time, Nan had a good friend named Sammy whom we'd nicknamed "Sambo." It wasn't meant to be derogatory and there was certainly no slur implied, it was just a play on the name, like "Jimbo" for Jim. Anyway, at the right point in the song that night I unfortunately transferred the affectionate nickname to Sammy Davis, without even thinking, and called out, "Hey Sambo, why don't you lead the mule train tonight?" He froze, stunned. I couldn't see him very well without my glasses and, thinking nothing was wrong, I turned to the other side of the room. Sammy stormed up to my conductor and tried to stop the music. He was restrained by his entourage, but he left the room in a rage and things were never the same between us again. All because of a very stupid, very innocent mistake.

If there's one thing I've never understood in my life, it's the ignorance that gives way to racism. When Nat Cole's television show was floundering because the network couldn't find anyone willing to sponsor a black man, I appeared on his show for nothing and many other white performers soon followed suit. I respected his talent, I loved the man, and he had been very nice to me when I was scuffling. As a return favor, Nat made a beautiful recording of a song I'd written with Freddy Karger, *Magnificent Obsession*.

As you can see, you gather all kinds of memories on the road. I still enjoy touring abroad and meeting new faces. I frequently play dates that take me back to England and Australia, and there are still a few new places I'd like to visit. *Desire* first caught fire over the Armed Forces Radio Network in Germany and Austria, and I regret that I've never spent as much time there as I'd like to. One of these days I'm going to have to find out how *Mule Train* plays in the Bavarian Alps.

* * * * * *

In November of 1966 I went to New York to work an extended engagement at a club out on Long Island. I was starting to wonder if I wasn't partially to blame for the recording rut I found myself in, so I thought that this might provide a good opportunity for Ray and me to work out some new arrangements and try some new stuff. That's

163

why we went out to Long Island. I had to go East to look around for a new record deal, but I didn't want to experiment with everyone watching at some place like the Copa. One evening a promoter from ABC-Paramount Records came in to catch the show. He put me in touch with a producer named Bob Thiele, and we arranged to have a meeting the next time I was in New York on business. Fifteen minutes after I met the guy, he was calling my agent on the West Coast and we had a deal.

The song they wanted me to record was *Every Street's a Boulevard in Old New York*, written for an old Dean Martin and Jerry Lewis movie by Bob Hilliard, the fellow who'd come up with *Moonlight Gambler* for me. The success of a revival of *Winchester Cathedral* had sparked an interest in 1920s-style music and they thought that *Boulevard* had the right feel to it to cash in. As a B-side, Bob suggested another old song called *Tomorrow*. I told him that if he wanted to go that route I had a better idea, and whipped out a song that I'd been carrying around with me for the past two years.

"What's this?," he asked.

"It's the theme song of all the Las Vegas hookers," I replied.

A few years before a friend of mine had asked me to stop off in Carson City, Nevada and visit a small club where a lady named Kay kept a big Wurlitzer juke box stocked with my old releases on 78rpm records. We had a pleasant chat and the next time I passed through on my way back from Reno I stopped in again. There was a sign hanging in the window that said "Closed Monday," When I asked the guy out front if I could speak to the owner, he said, "I'm the owner." His name was Bill Porter and he'd just bought the place from Kay.

When he realized who I was he took me inside to an organ which he'd installed to entertain the customers. He said there was a song he sang every night that would be just perfect for me, and then launched into one of the worst renditions of a piece of music I've ever heard in my life. Ever so gradually, the melody filtered through and I asked him to play it for me again. I'd never heard the tune before, but something about it grabbed me. I had Bill send me a tape of the song, which was called *I'll Take Care of Your Cares*, and when I got home I began searching for the publisher.

I couldn't find the song listed anywhere, not even in the ASCAP catalogue. This struck me as a good omen, because the last song I'd had that problem with was *That's My Desire*. A friend of my manager's finally tracked down the sheet music and it turned out to be a waltz, written in the mid-'20s by Dixon and Monaco. Bill Porter had worked it up into a fox-trot, and we in turn jazzed up his version into a real swinging song for me. Before I got ahold of it, the song was best known as an anthem for Nevada's fallen women and was stocked in juke boxes all over Las Vegas.

The brass at Capitol wouldn't let me record it, so I carried the music around in my pocket for two years. Pete De Angelis worked up a great arrangement for the song at ABC, and when everyone heard it they all agreed that *Cares* had to be the A-side of my first release. Like *Desire*, it was recorded near year's end and got lost in the Christmas music until early the following year. By February, 1967, it started getting a lot of attention. Pretty soon it topped all the easy listening charts and we were back in business. *Cares* was the first in a string of nine hits in a row at ABC which culminated for me in 1969 with *Lord, You Gave Me A Mountain*.

The tempo of *Cares* had a sing-along feel to it that we duplicated in two more successful records, *Making Memories* and *You Wanted Someone To Play With*. We shifted gears with the next release, a terrific country ballad by

Leon Ashley and Margie Singleton called *Laura, What's He Got That I Ain't Got?* I was picking good material and getting lucky with it again. I should have known it was too good to last.

I make it a practice never to speak ill of anybody, especially publicly, but I must confess that I've seldom disliked a fellow human being as much as I did Larry Newton, the President of ABC. He's one of the few persons I can honestly say that I met and detested immediately. To his mind, every song had to sound exactly like *I'll Take Care of Your Cares* or he didn't want to put it out. His attitude began to grate on my nerves. After the eighth sound-a-like in a row, I tried to reason with him.

"Look Larry," I pleaded, "Two or three in a row from the same mold is fine, but you run your string on these things. Soon every song sounds like the one before it, each one sells less than the one before it, and you're down to nothing. You're cutting your own throat. If there's one thing I learned from Mitch Miller, it's that you've got to change direction with your material."

He waved his hand contemptuously and sneered, "Ah, the hell with Mitch."

"No," I shot back furiously, "the hell with *you!*"

A song had come into my office that was pure magic. The great Marty Robbins had written it with me in mind. I wasn't going to let some narrow-minded executive rob me of the chance to do it justice, and I refused to get burned again the way I had with *The Impossible Dream*. This song was just too right.

I believed in *Lord, You Gave Me A Mountain* so strongly that I was ready to get an independent producer and go after it all alone.

TWELVE

YOU GAVE ME A MOUNTAIN

Marty Robbins once told me that he'd been trying to bring *Lord, You Gave Me A Mountain* to my attention for several years before he finally succeeded in November, 1968. I wish he'd been quicker about it. There were many times in the mid-60s when I longed for a song of its quality.

As I listened to the first four bars of the demo tape he sent I was struck by the way it conjured up memories of *Lucky Old Sun* and *I Believe*. I think Marty crafted the lyric that way deliberately. There was one line in the lyric, though, that bothered me. It went: "Despised and ignored by my father."

My father had just died in September, and he and I adored each other. The first thing I could think of to do when I started earning big money was to retire him to a house with lots of ground for gardening, which he loved to do. I just couldn't sing a line about a "despising father" with conviction, so Marty let me alter it to "Deprived of the love of my father." Still, every time I reached that line it brought back mental images of Pa in his casket and they broke me up inside. *Mountain* remains a difficult number for me to get through today. It's ironic that my career got a second wind from a song that fills me with sadness.

After I laid down the law to Larry Newton, telling him I was going to record this song whether he liked it or not, I turned to Jimmy Haskell (one of the best writers on the West Coast) for an arrangement. Then I got in touch with Jimmy Bowen and asked him to be my producer. Our record was released without any help from ABC or Larry Newton. No fanfare, no promotion, no nothing. In spite of that, it shot into the top ten in 1969. We didn't make it to number one because of some stiff competition from Sinatra's *My Way* and a couple of songs by Glen Campbell, who was very hot at the time. But it was a big hit record, later covered by Elvis Presley, among others, and a lot of people who had written me off were shrugging their shoulders and saying, "Well, he did it again!"

It reminded me of a play by Pirandello that I'd read a long time ago when I was a schoolboy back in Chicago. He said that nothing in life can remain at a white hot intensity because it would burn itself out. Every time you hit a peak, you cool off. I've tried to keep that in mind throughout my career and my personal life. It's helped me to see the highs and lows of experience as part of a larger picture. Rick Marlow, the guy who wrote *A Taste Of Honey*, had been a roommate of mine at one point during the lean years. When he first heard *Mountain* on the radio he called to tell me he thought I had another evergreen. He was right. It's become one of the two or three songs that I have to include in every show.

Like *I Believe*, the lyrics touched people with their message of faith in a higher power. I think affirmation of this faith is so important to a happy life that I once sat down and wrote to Governors, Congressmen, and Mayors all across the country suggesting that a Saturday and Sunday in May be set aside as annual "I Believe Days." The response was very positive, and Congressman Thomas M.

Rees from California kindly read some supportive remarks into the Congressional Record on May 4, 1970. I'd like to see people make such days a regular occasion for looking forward with hope to a brighter future.

After *Mountain* I didn't want to record with ABC anymore. I enjoyed working with Jimmy Bowen so much that I left to join him at a fledgling little company he'd started called Amos Records. We decided to begin our association with a look back. The early '70s seemed like a good time to re-record some of my old standards, putting a contemporary spin on them.

We worked up some great new charts for *Desire, Shine,* and eight others. They designed a really beautiful fold-out album cover with a montage of pictures from my early days. Nobody could decide on a clever title, though, and I felt too close to the project to try. I left the decision in the hands of Bruce Hinton, who ran the business side of Amos. Would you believe he prevailed upon everybody to call it *Frankie Laine's Greatest Hits*? At this time the only two albums Columbia was still selling were *Hell Bent For Leather* and *Frankie Laine's Greatest Hits*. If you went into a record store and asked for my greatest hits, without specifically mentioning the Amos label, chances are you'd be handed my Columbia album, which was originally released in 1958. The confusion between the two records defeated the whole purpose, which was to introduce new versions of the songs to a new generation of listeners.

We tried again with an album called *A Brand New Day.* In those sessions we concentrated completely on songs by new writers and powerful contemporary material like *Put Your Hand in the Hand, Mr. Bojangles,* and John Fogerty's terrific *Proud Mary.* It turned out to be a fine album, one of my personal favorites, but financial difficulties with other projects sent the Amos label down the drain. We had an amiable parting and I returned my attention to concert appearances.

With Tony Martin and Cyd Charisse.

With Dorothy McGuire and Deborah Kerr at a rehearsal.

* * * * * *

During this period I'd become addicted to a new hobby, and for a long time every spare minute was spent on the ocean, sportfishing with Nan.

It all started with a 1961 vacation we took in La Paz, Mexico. To try something different we went on a fishing expedition. That very afternoon Nan caught a black marlin and I landed a sailfish. From then on we were hooked. We moved from Beverly Hills to Malibu to be nearer the water, and ended up taking so many trips down to San Diego for the marvelous fishing there that we moved to that beautiful city full time in 1968. It's a testimony to my love of the sport that I used to go out so often in spite of the fact that I was incurably seasick. No pill in the world could help me and I suffered terribly until they came up with the transderm patch, which you can place behind the ear to steady your equilibrium.

We got commercial fishing licenses in 1971 and decided the next year that the time had come to build our own boat, a forty-six footer we christened the good ship *My Desire*. That first summer after it was built was marvelous fun. We caught sixty swordfish, five of them weighing in at over 500 pounds. People don't realize the good shape you need to be in to wrestle something that heavy. I once fought a Pacific Blue Marlin for four hours, and for the rest of the afternoon after we brought him in my arms hung at my sides like a couple of wet noodles.

The touring gave us a chance to visit some of the best sportfishing locales in the world. The waters off Cape Town, South Africa, provided some particularly challenging moments. In the fall of 1974, a friend organized a Frankie Laine Billfish Classic for the benefit of the Damon Runyon Cancer Fund in Fort Lauderdale, Florida, with celebrity fishermen like Jonathan Winters and Lee Marvin.

For me, part of the attraction of fishing was the relaxed, informal atmosphere around the docks. I loved to hang around in casual clothes (actually, more like beaten up, tattered clothes), and both Nan and I were shocked when the Custom Tailors Guild of America selected me as one of the ten best dressed men in the country two years in a row. If their membership had seen us lounging around the deck, they would have unanimously demanded a recall. I was just a regular boat slob.

* * * * * *

Without a record contract in 1971, I began spending more time in Las Vegas than ever before.

I've always enjoyed playing Vegas, but more than one doctor has told me, "I think you singers are crazy for going there!" Two shows a night in that dry desert air can play absolute hell with your throat. Another thing that used to bother me there was a little voice in the back of my head that kept telling me there was a mathematical possibility that I was playing to an audience of 600 losers. How do you entertain a room full of 600 losers? On the lighter side, you can joke and kid around with a Vegas audience more intimately than you can in a concert hall. When I decided to grow back my *"Moonlight Gambler* beard," I polled the audience every night for an approval rating. I fibbed and told them I was growing the foliage to play the Alfred Drake role in *Kismet*. They liked the beard, sixty percent to forty, so it stayed.

The drawbacks of playing Las Vegas are smoothed over by the kind of money they pay you, but the memory of my vocal problems in the early fifties still haunted me and when the bouts of "desert throat" started getting too severe I started looking for someplace else to go. The answer came my way in September, 1973, when I ran across Dr. Mac Robinson (then the head of my English fan club) in New York. He was visiting with his American counterpart, John Lambrosa, who at that time was running the national club out of Rochester, New York.

Mac argued that after so much time away I should give serious consideration to touring England again. Between shuffling record labels and extending my concert tours to new and different areas, I'd neglected to set foot on British soil for the past seventeen years. Mac said that the fans couldn't understand why I'd stayed away so long and gave me a spiel about how "once the English people take you to their hearts they never give you up" (which is very true). It was a year before we were able to schedule a series of dates for a four-week tour. I had no idea what sort of reception would be waiting for me and I decided that if we bombed, a month wouldn't be that hard to live with. We'd be out of there in no time.

To my relief, the greatest reception I've ever had at any club anywhere was on opening night, November, 1974, at Blighty's Club in Manchester. The place was jammed with two thousand screaming maniacs. When I got on stage the shouting, stomping, and whistling was so loud that I couldn't hear the music. I didn't know where Ray Barr was, and the last thing I wanted to do after seventeen years away was make a wrong entrance on the very first song. I stopped the music, walked up to the microphone, and said, "Thank you very much. I love you for this, but I can't hear the music." They got such a kick out of that, they became twice as loud! The warmth and affection washed over the footlights in waves all night long, and it was the same story with every remaining stop on the tour.

In 1975 we went back for another eight weeks. I was contacted by the BBC early in June, a week before the last stop in Plymouth. An executive named Peter Scott was interested in producing a television show with me. We shot it in Manchester, and it was beautifully done. No dancers, singers or any of that glitzy production b.s. It was just me and the orchestra in an intimate setting with a studio audience. I did my own announcements and kept the patter between songs to a minimum so they could fit in as much music as possible. We did a fourteen song set which closed with *Kid's Last Fight*, a million seller that had been extremely popular there and in South Africa. The whole show ran forty-one minutes, an oddball time, but they don't watch the clock over there like we do in the States. It's looser and more relaxed. I like it that way.

After we finished they told me it would likely be edited and ready to air in a month. When I got home and August, September, and October passed by without a word from England, I decided that maybe they didn't like what we'd done. This depressed me because I knew the show was too good to just junk or leave gathering dust on a shelf somewhere. It would also have made wonderful advance publicity for the return visit we were contemplating in 1976, but I adopted a defensive posture about the whole thing and told those who asked, "Ah, the hell with it. I don't care if they never play it."

What I didn't know was that one of the BBC programmers had liked the show so much that they were holding it back to use as a special on New Year's Day, one of the top viewing days of the year. It ended up with some of the highest ratings, outside of a sporting event, of any show they've had over there.

Since then I've made many return visits and recorded two albums, *Life is Beautiful* (the title track was a great song written by Fred Astaire) and *20 Memories in Gold*, for the Polydor label in London. In March of 1988, a hundred members of my ever-loyal British fan club flew out to San Diego to help me celebrate my 75th birthday. Their gesture added a nice touch to my continuing love affair with the country I've long considered to be my second professional home.

* * * * * *

Right before that first return trip to England, twenty-one years after *Blowing Wild* in 1953, I had the opportunity to make my seventh film title song. It was a strange job, and it came about in a strange way.

I'd just finished singing *Wild Goose* during a guest appearance on *The Merv Griffin Show,* which was taping in Las Vegas. When I got back to my hotel there was a message waiting asking me to call a guy named Mel Brooks. The name didn't ring a bell, but I called him anyway and he said that he'd just finished a movie at Warner Brothers called *Blazing Saddles* and he wanted me to sing the theme song (Mel later told me that after he saw the Griffin show he jumped up and shouted, "That's the guy who should do our song!"). He said he needed to have the song in a week, but I was in the middle of a two week engagement in Vegas and tried to beg off until after it was over. I told him about the hard tone I get when I record while working clubs, but he said that was **exactly** the quality he wanted for the record. Two days later he had me on a plane to Hollywood.

We made eight takes of the song. I thought the seventh one was it. I'd been learning the thing as I went along during the previous six, figuring out what to add and what to delete. We did an eighth take because Mel said, "You never know what might happen to the tape," but it was the seventh take that ended up in the movie. I was happy to get worldwide distribution with another film soundtrack, but when I finally saw the completed picture at an exhibitor's show in South Africa, I was stunned.

This may sound ridiculous, but nobody had told me this film was a comedy. I guess everyone just assumed I knew, but I didn't. I was unfamiliar with Mel Brooks and his reputation. I thought I was doing a song for another *High Noon*, and I gave it my best dramatic reading. When I saw wacky things happening on the screen, like a guy punching a horse, I sunk down into my seat with embarrassment. The comedy gave the record an unintended tongue-in-cheek quality, and everything worked out fine. It even sold fairly well as a single.

* * * * * *

The next project I tackled was probably too far ahead of its time. While I was still with ABC, Jack Lawrence, a great songwriter who has a couple of hundred copyrights to his name (*If I Didn't Care* and *Linda*, among them), brought me a special piece of material he'd put together called *Talk to Me 'Bout the Hard Times*. The song spoke of the trouble and misery one man had witnessed through the course of his long life, and I could personally identify with many parts of it. It had a tricky, cyclical vocal that was nine minutes long, the longest I'd ever heard of in popular music history. I knew that Larry Newton would never let me try something as offbeat as that. It was also a dark, Depression song, and at the time the country was in the midst of Lyndon Johnson's "Great Society" euphoria. The timing was all wrong.

By the mid-seventies, I was free from ABC and the economy had taken a big turn for the worse. In the meantime, Studs Terkel had written a best-seller called *Hard Times* and Charles Bronson had made a movie called *The Hard Times*. I started digging around in my files and found a tape of Jack's song without the vocal. I also found a paper with the lyrics on it. I tried to make the two of them come together through repeated listenings, but it was too long and complicated. I couldn't remember where the lyrics came in and I couldn't remember where to lay out.

During a tour of England I ran across Jack's publisher, Lou Levy, and asked him to have Jack send me the music and a demo tape with his voice on it so I could piece the whole thing together. When I got back I couldn't wait to get my hands on it. Nan, who I hadn't seen for eight weeks, was a little miffed. "What the hell are you so excited about?" she demanded. I had her sit down and listen to the song with me and she said, "Gee honey, that's a fantastic piece of material, but how long was it?" We played it through again to time it and discovered it ran nine minutes and thirty-two seconds.

For the better part of the next two months, every time we returned to shore after a fishing trip and every time I drove to Los Angeles on business, I popped that cassette into a player and studied it, trying to determine how to put my own individual stamp on something that intricate. In November of 1975 I felt ready to take a shot at it. Like with *Foreign Affair*, the playback told me there were spots that could be improved. Three weeks later I tried it again, and this time Jack and I agreed that we had what we wanted.

It was too different for any of the major labels to gamble on. We ended up placing it with a jazz label called Mainstream Records, and they released it in early 1976. Some disc jockeys in the U.S. and Canada who'd been boosters of mine for a long time tried to give it generous air play but, unfortunately, most stations didn't want to touch a ten-minute song. One of the most artistically satisfying projects I'd ever completed proved to be one of the least commercial things I've ever recorded.

Everything is relative, though. I remembered back to the mid-'50s when Mitch Miller brought me a number called *Ticky Ticky Tick*. It was a novelty song, and quite honestly, it stunk. "But Frank," Mitch pleaded, "I brought you *I Believe!*" I made the record, and the results were embarrassing. At home my daughters asked, "Daddy, how could you?" I told them, "But girls, he brought me *I Believe!*" I was riding a wave then, and that record probably outsold *Hard Times* ten times over, but there's no debate about which effort made me prouder.

You have to be able to measure achievement with other tools besides a cash register.

In concert.

THIRTEEN

MAKING MORE MEMORIES

A short time ago, I participated in a special on Public Television that celebrated the music of the early '50s. After it aired, I received a nice letter from a fan who closed by saying, "I'm so glad you're back in action. You should never retire." Who retired? I never have retired and I never will, but when people haven't seen you around they often jump to a false conclusion. If I go on tour in England or South Africa for eight weeks, I'll invariably come back to the States and run across somebody in New York who asks, "Where the hell have you been? We thought you'd retired." I'm not even semi-retired. I just limit my time on the road these days, and have always made it a point to stop and smell the roses along the way.

As long ago as the late '50s I started to work out less demanding touring schedules, and now I try to keep the travel down to just 15 weeks out of the year. Health and age have nothing to do with it. If I worked 20 weeks, pretty soon I'd be under pressure to do 30, and why should I push myself? I don't see any point in success if you can't break away and enjoy the fruits of your labor. A cozy evening at home with a good book for company is an indulgence, and I've earned it. I enjoy horseback riding, golf, sportfishing, and coin collecting, and have toyed with all of them over the years. I even took a fling at oil painting, but Nan has all the talent in that department. I hope someday to find time to play a little classical guitar, another pursuit I've noodled with for many years.

None of these pastimes, however, mean that my passion for performing has in any way diminished over the years. I take a genuine joy in communicating with an audience. When the audience loves what you do, that joy is greatly multiplied. No two shows are ever the same, because no two audiences are ever exactly alike. Some people ask me how I can stand to sing the same numbers night after night, and I tell them that the song is kept fresh by the different people who come in to hear it each time. I give it my best shot at every show, because you never know who might be out front. The bottom line is that it's somebody who's parted with some hard earned money to see me perform, and that implies a strong commitment on my part. I always try to hold up my end of the bargain.

Many people think that older entertainers have too much of the ham in them, and are compelled by ego to stay out there in front of the crowds. Speaking for myself, I just can't imagine what else I would do. I'd be the first to quit if I knew I wasn't sounding good or thought that people weren't interested in hearing from me any more. That hasn't happened yet, and hopefully it never will. A big part of you has to die when you give up the thing you love best.

When fans write and tell me how *Desire* or *We'll Be Together Again* or *I Believe* has affected their lives, I'm deeply gratified. It's a marvel to me how these songs can touch people in ways that no one could have foreseen when they were recorded. A disc jockey friend of mine returned from a vacation in Montana and told me that he'd met a twenty-seven year old cowboy out there who knows all my western things by heart, and sings them to himself for company while he rides the range. In a little town called Mule Shoe, Texas, they have a program called *The Mule Train News* which they open and close by playing my record. In Japan, they liked *Rawhide* so much that Suntory Scotch Whiskey made it the focus of an advertising campaign.

My dearest memory of how a simple song can touch people occurred during the 1954 tour of England. The Command Performance was an incredible professional thrill, but the personal highlight for me was the time I spent with a little six year old girl named Jean Hancox. Her feet were amputated after a street car accident, and for a while the doctors feared for her life. They gave her artificial limbs, and learning to walk on them was a traumatic ordeal for her. While she was convalescing she would listen to *Frankie Laine Time*, a show that was broadcast over Radio Luxembourg. She wrote to tell me that my songs (particularly her favorite, *Wild Goose*) had helped her to forget her pain. When I got to Sheffield I visited Jean at home, and later at the theater we played catch in my dressing room. Watching that darling, brave little child in a pink ballerina dress with a ribbon in her hair, squealing and giggling as she ran across the carpet after a ball, I was as happy as I've ever been.

While I'm on the subject, I have to share with you a letter that came in shortly after my second bypass operation. I'll let it speak for itself, exactly as written, and just add that it's one of my most prized possessions:

19 April 1990

HEY FRANKIE BABY..............

GET WELL, YOU'RE THE GREATEST

In 1968 when I was a prisoner of war in Viet Nam, they used to play music to make us homesick. I was Navy, and the guy in the cell next to me was just a young kid about 20 or so, and naturally a ROCK FAN. He was a marine. Anyway ... he used to shout at the V.C. and tell them to stop playing that damn FRANKIE LAINE MUSIC. Well, I was about 37 then and I grew up with your music and your great voice. So I would yell back and tell the BASTARDS that if they stopped playing your music, I would never confess to war crimes.

Well. . . they figured that I might just do it, so they played you a lot. Doris Day, Sarah Vaughn, and Nancy Wilson were others that helped a lot. But the best was you and ME singing our lungs out while the V.C. just smiled and thought I was cracking up.

To this day I don't think they knew how much you helped me over the most difficult time in my life. To this day when I hear you on my car radio going down the freeway, I sing like hell and scare the crap out of people. Sometimes, at a red light, some guy will yell over and say, "Hey you, you ain't no Frankie Laine!"

I JUST SMILE AND SAY GOD BLESS HIM. THANK GOD FOR FRANKIE LAINE. GET WELL FRANKIE.... WE NEED YA.

Carl D. Jay
Chief Petty Officer
U.S. Navy Retired.

It took a long time, but music eventually brought me success, security, and some priceless "fringe benefits" like that. For me, it will always be the only game in town.

* * * * * *

The 1980s began with a look back to the very beginning, well before even *That's My Desire*, back to the days when I was singing and starving at the same time. A recording studio engineer named Wally Heider came across a set of Frankie Laine transcription discs that had been tossed on the shelf at a little radio station in Oregon and forgotten about for forty years. Even I'd forgotten that these recordings existed. They were made for a transcription service in Los Angeles that wanted me to do a bunch of standards for them. At these sessions I recorded songs like *Lady Be Good* and *You Can Depend On Me*, plus alternate versions of records I later made at Mercury. All of this material was discovered unopened, in its original packaging. We had audio technicians bring the sound quality up to modern day standards, and then Wally and I divided up the tunes for release. He came up with a couple of albums entitled *The Uncollected Frankie Laine* on Hindsight Records, and I released one called *So Ultra Rare* on my own Score Records label.

The response was fantastic. Even people who'd been collecting my stuff from day one didn't have this material, and the releases helped flesh out my recording catalogue and gave everyone a better idea of what I sounded like during the hungry years.

We followed up *So Ultra Rare* with another visit to my musical "roots," so to speak. Arranger Jimmy Namaro updated the charts on some of the jazz standards I'd missed along the way. We mixed in the results with some new material and released it as a jazz album entitled *Place in Time*. Then I went to Nashville to record my first real country album, *A Country Laine*.

I'd recorded a lot of country music before, but those records were always marketed as pop releases. In fact, I've yet to be "blessed" by the powers that be in Nashville as an authentic country singer. I think that's because even when I work with country and western material, I can't fully let go of my jazz roots. In 1982 when I recorded a song called *Texas*, many listeners arched their eyebrows and said it was the first time they'd ever heard somebody scat sing a country song.

I keep trying, though. In 1987 I cut a compact disc with Erich Kunzel and the Cincinnati Pops Orchestra entitled *Round-Up*. It was a collection of Wild West themes and musical Americana, and it went to number four on *Billboard's* Classical Music chart. One place I never expected to see myself was on the classical music charts! It was a rattling experience to perform those songs while facing 87 concert musicians. It's probably the only time my hand ever shook while I turned the pages of sheet music. I've always enjoyed the rich, full backing you get from a symphony orchestra, and for years I've appeared regularly with the symphonies in New Orleans, St. Louis, Cleveland, Atlanta, Rochester, San Francisco, and elsewhere all across the country.

Whether you're appearing with a full symphony orchestra or a three-piece combo, few people are more important to a singer than the arranger/accompanist. That's the person who makes sure you're given the musical support you need, and in my career I've been blessed with the best. After Carl's untimely passing, six years went by before I found another musical soul mate in Ray Barr. We stayed together for twenty-one years, far longer than I worked with anyone else, and only his death in 1983 had the power to interrupt an indissoluble partnership. In July of '83 I hired Jimmy Namaro to follow in Ray's footsteps. Jimmy is a silver haired gentleman from Canada, so we jokingly refer to him on stage as the "Toronto Flash." He's a true professional, and I am fortunate to be working with him.

One of Ray's last contributions proved to be a revelation to all of us. During our 1982 tour of England, we were having trouble fitting all of the songs the fans wanted to hear into our set. There just wasn't time for them all, but English fans tend to be very vocal about their disappointments. If you don't include every song they came to hear, and I mean **every** song, they don't hesitate to let you know about it before you leave the stage. Ray decided to arrange the biggest hits into a medley, and he fit in twelve extra songs by cutting the middle out of each tune. Everyone was pleased, and the kicker is that nobody noticed that anything was different. When we tried out the medley back home, the results were the same. I don't think many people realized that we'd tampered with the songs.

When I think of all the time I've wasted singing those extra half-choruses for nothing!

* * * * * *

I'm grateful to be able to say that in the '80s the fans were still clamoring for more elsewhere throughout Europe. During the late '70s and early '80s, I made several re-recordings of the old songs for "Greatest Hits" packages on foreign labels. The most memorable among them was the session I did for Arcade Records, which was headquartered in Holland (the Arcade Theater in Amsterdam has always been one of my favorite venues to play). These people wanted the results to sound as much like the original records as possible, so they sent me a cassette of the songs they'd picked and for three months I listened to it and had the strange experience of re-learning the tunes from myself.

We went to Nashville in January of 1981 and cut twenty selections which they packaged and marketed as *The World of Frankie Laine*. We used the best musicians available, and the mood in the studio was very upbeat. Everyone was still basking in the glow of the recent holiday season. The good time we had while recording must have come through on the album. When it was released in '82, it topped the charts in Holland and earned me another gold record.

Back on the "home" front, Nan and I finally found the ideal site for the house of our dreams. San Diego is one of the most beautiful towns I've ever seen. We picked a spot high atop a sandstone cliff in the Point Loma area with a panoramic view of the city and its harbor. With the logistic help of some local builders, Nan designed the house herself.

This was a good outlet for her tremendous creative drive, which she's channeled into a variety of areas since leaving the movies. Not many people know that besides acting, Nan is also an inventor. In the '60s she was responsible for the invention of the magnifying cosmetic mirror, which has proved helpful to ladies around the world. When she began marketing her invention, one of her first customers was the late Princess Grace of Monaco.

It took two years after the ground breaking on June 15, 1983, to get the new house built. There were cost overruns and delays galore. For the longest time, I was up to my ass in architects. It was important to get it right, because we knew that most of our leisure time would be spent there. We accept only the occasional invitation these days (we went through the "party circuit" scene years ago), and it surprises many to learn that very few of our closest friends are involved with show business. One of the main reasons we moved to San Diego, aside from the fishing, was to escape from the "I just care about myself and the hell with everybody else" mentality that pervades so much of Hollywood. I can't stand that kind of crap, and I don't fool around with those kinds of people.

Nan and I are as pleased with each other's company today as we were forty years ago. I think the main reason our marriage has weathered the decades so well is that we've always had a lot of respect for each other and for each other's individuality. Four simple points govern our lives together:

1) Live and let live

2) To each his own

3) Do unto others as you would have others do unto you

4) All things in moderation

The phrases are cliches, but their simple truths are valid. If more people would show more regard for their partner's feelings I don't think that lasting marriages, particularly show business ones, would be such a rare phenomenon.

* * * * * *

I've been a lucky old son, it's true, but nothing worthwhile in my life has ever come without a price or a struggle. Our dream home proved to be no exception. While unpacking some crates that had been delivered to the new house, I experienced a sharp pain in the chest that eventually parlayed itself into the frightening ordeal of quadruple bypass heart surgery.

With my accompanist for 21 years, Ray Barr.

Frankie and Nan today.

FOURTEEN

PLACE IN TIME

After the operation Nan spent restless nights watching over me, just as Terry Fischer had done for Carl some thirty years before. Mercifully, that's where the parallel ends. I was fortunate enough to survive my ordeal, though I was left to wonder whether our new house might end up being my "retirement home" after all. I knew that I didn't want it to be, but no one could be certain that I'd have any choice in the matter.

The bumpy road that leads to recovery from heart surgery was made much smoother by the many cards and letters of support I received from kindhearted people all over the world. I had plenty of time to sit and read them, too, because of some complications that arose after the surgery. I was given a drug called Heparin to thin my blood before the operation, and another one called Protamine to return it to normal clotting. Only about one in 300 patients proves allergic to Protamine. I turned out to be one of the unlucky few. My skin rippled until it looked like goose flesh, and I retained so much of the water which they used to flush out my system that I bloated up to 255 pounds. Eleven days later I'd lost fifty of those pounds, and felt well enough to begin my recuperation period at home.

I used to tell fitness fanatics that two shows a night was all the exercise I ever needed, but after the operation I had to change my lifestyle and my diet. I took a twelve-week cardiac rehabilitation course at Mercy Hospital, learned about proper nutrition, and was encouraged to start a regular walking program. Soon I was feeling better than I had in years. I began tentatively humming my favorite songs while puttering around the new house, and after three months the voice was back. I banished all my fears of enforced retirement, at least for a while, and resumed a full schedule of recording dates and personal appearances.

I got five good years out of that first operation. Then, in the beginning of 1990, I started experiencing brief attacks of angina again and instinct told me more trouble lay ahead. There were some guest appearances with symphony orchestras on my immediate schedule, and a four-week tour of England had been set up for June. I decided it would be wise to have my doctors check out the situation first, but I wanted to wait until after I'd fulfilled a special commitment.

In the summer of '89, I'd promised to go to St. Louis the following spring to help the symphony with a benefit celebrating the 70th birthday of Richard Hayman, the conductor of their summer pops series. Richard had been a good friend; St. Louis has always been a great town for me, and I was looking forward to working again with the talented musicians there. It wasn't meant to be.

On the trip over I experienced a sharp angina pain while catching my connecting flight in Dallas. I took a nitro and laid low until I arrived in St. Louis late in the afternoon on March 26. The concert was set for the following evening. Unfortunately, three nitro pills couldn't keep the angina from returning three more times in the early morning hours on the day of the show. When you experience that kind of recurring pain while you're at rest, it's time to get help. I had the hotel desk call the paramedics, who whisked me to a hospital.

To my everlasting appreciation, St. Louis University Hospital is a first-rate institution with a very caring, attentive staff that took wonderful care of me. An angiogram showed that my situation was unstable and Nan flew out to be by my side. While the physicians were balancing the possible need for surgery there in St. Louis against the stress I might experience flying home to my own doctors, the equation got a little more complicated when I came down with a case of bronchitis.

Fortunately, during this time a Medivac plane that had flown a cardiac patient from San Diego to Houston became available for the return trip. On April 4 an ambulance took me to the airport. The two Medivac pilots, Nan, an attending nurse, and I all piled on board. Four and a half hours later I was back home in San Diego and once again in Mercy Hospital. They gave me some antibiotics and waited six days for the bronchitis to clear up (that frightening sense of urgency that went with my first operation was mercifully out of the picture this time). On April 10 Dr. Houseman performed a successful triple bypass with no complications.

I've talked with many different people who've undergone "redos" and heard all kinds of opinions: it's easier/harder the second time around; it's more/less painful. In my own experience, the physical pain was just as bad if not worse the second time around, but a good deal of the mental strain and that nagging fear of the unknown is gone when you've been there before. Also, this second time I was spared some of the unpleasantness that followed on the heels of my first operation, like severe insomnia and

With Walter Winchell and Bob Hope.

bouts of depression. It just goes to prove that it's hard to keep a lucky old son down!

I thank God every day for my good fortune and I like to try, in my own small way, to give something back. Shortly after Carl Fischer's death, I wanted to increase my charity workload. Walter Winchell recruited me to join forces with the Damon Runyon Cancer Fund, and I'm proud to say that our association is still going strong today.

One night Nan and I were watching the news on television when a segment on homelessness showed some poor guy being rousted from a park bench. He had big holes in the soles of his shoes, and it started me thinking. Everyone always talks about food and clothes for the needy, but no one seems to think about shoes, and so many of the homeless are on their feet all day and all night. I called Don Howard (a San Diego disc jockey at radio station KPOP) the next morning and told him I'd like to become involved somehow with a shoe drive. He asked if there was a song somewhere in my repertoire that we might use as theme music. I was about to tell him no when

I remembered with a sudden jolt that back in 1955 I'd cut a song for a Columbia single entitled *Old Shoes*. It was a good tune that had been lost in the onslaught of rock and roll. I tracked it down in my music library and gave it a listen. The lyrics suited our needs perfectly.

We had our first "Shoes for the Homeless" drive over the 1990 holiday season and managed to collect 6,000 pairs of shoes in San Diego County alone. Since then, the idea has spread to Cincinnati, Portland, San Francisco, and elsewhere. I've enlisted the support of the Salvation Army and other civic groups, and I've performed at several benefit concerts where a pair of old shoes was tacked onto the price of admission. I'm genuinely enthusiastic about this *Old Shoes* campaign. It has the potential to do a lot of good. If you'll pardon the expression, we might even save a few soles along the way.

I've also been involved with the "Meals on Wheels" program, and with other groups that are concerned with the welfare of our nation's senior citizens. I can't help but think that if my career hadn't panned out, I'd be numbered today among our many older citizens who live in loneliness, fear, need, and neglect. When I was a kid, the elderly didn't have the kind of help available to them that they do today. I'd like to see more seniors take advantage of it and enjoy peace of mind in their later years.

My surname, LoVecchio, means "The Old One" in Italian. When people talk to me about aging, I like to borrow a line from Maurice Chevalier and remind them that "it's better than the alternative." Age is essentially a state of mind. The only thing truly difficult about the passing years are all the good people you lose along the way. None of the three men I dedicated this autobiography to, for example, are still around to read it.

In 1984, Ma died after a "brief" six-week illness. Six weeks seems more like an eternity when you're losing your mother. She was ninety years old, and I'm grateful that she did not suffer. Her love and support made all the difference for me in the beginning, and I'm glad that I had her company to enjoy for as long as I did. (Nan and I had to go through a similar ordeal when we lost her mother in December, 1986.)

In 1985 my sister, Gloria, contracted cancer of the throat, and I was the only relative left on the West Coast who could help. I made regular trips to Los Angeles to comfort and care for her, but she didn't pull through. My brothers Sam, Joe, and John had all passed on before her.

On return trips to Chicago, I used to enjoy having dinner and reminiscing with my sister, Rose, and my brother, Phil. We lost Rose in 1991, and now my baby brother and I are all that's left out of the nine people who once added up to a very happy and close knit LoVecchio clan back in the '20s. Few things can make you more melancholy or misty-eyed than silent, empty chairs around the old family table.

* * * * * *

As times change tastes change with them, and a singer has to accommodate both if he or she hopes to stay around. I know that a lot of my contemporaries dismiss all modern popular music as garbage, but I think my old friend Woody Herman had a better attitude when he noted that there are just two kinds of music: good and bad. Some of today's pop is terrific, some of it is junk, but it has progressed far beyond what we were hearing when rock first hit the scene.

In the mid-'50s, a lot of kids ran out and started bands without first mastering their instruments. Rock fell into a kind of rut in which the same basic three chords were used over and over again because the kids couldn't handle anything more complex. The songs all started to sound the same. As with anything new, things improved over time and eventually you saw people like Bob Dylan, the

Beatles, Paul Simon, and Neil Diamond, to name but a few, turning out fantastic pieces of contemporary material.

I don't think that the kind of music these people produced should be called "rock." I feel it's progressed beyond that point, and I like to refer to them as contemporary writers, just to differentiate them from the more traditional school of popular song writing. If they were writing today, I don't know if a Hoagy Carmichael or an Irving Berlin could turn out a song like *Bridge Over Troubled Waters*. They just wouldn't feel the music the same way.

Neither the newer or older styles are inherently better. They're just different. I listen to all types of music from many different eras today. The only genre that I've discovered I can't deal with is "heavy metal," because there's no distinguishable melodic pattern.

I also don't like gimmicky acts. You can't be very talented if you have to dye your hair pink and green to get attention. For me, the bottom line is still: if you can't come away humming the song, it probably needs work.

* * * * * *

People who want to sing for a living are coming to me all the time for advice, and my message for them is straight and to the point — **"WORK!"**

Singing is a craft that's mastered by doing, watching, practicing, and listening. You can't deliberately sit down and create an individual style. Just do what feels right to you and a personal style will evolve naturally over time. Everyone starts out being influenced by somebody else.

In the late '40s, for example, the innovative songwriting team of Freddie Katz and Jack Wilson brought me a marvelous piece of material entitled *Satan Wears A Satin Gown* (I later recorded it, but the song never caught on. It had a complex structure and offbeat lyric that I think was too far ahead of its time). Freddie brought with him a singer named Joe Bari. When the two of them finished demonstrating the song I asked, "What the hell do you need me for? This guy sings great!" Joe glumly confessed that he wasn't recording and added, "I'm not signed up for the same reason *you* weren't recording a few years ago. Nobody wants me." I knew exactly where he was coming from.

Joe stuck with it and eventually became a label mate of mine at Columbia. He emulated my style on his first few recordings and then Percy Faith, a great arranger and conductor, took him aside and suggested that he try and find his own, unique voice. When Joe did, he became a top selling artist. Shortly before signing with Columbia, he also changed his stage name to Tony Bennett.

Another piece of advice I give the starry-eyed types is to find another way to earn a living until music starts paying off. There have to be better roads to travel than the seventeen-year route I took, but success never comes easily. My courage failed me several times along the way. When I hear young musicians complaining that they've been trying "for a whole year" and nothing's happened with their careers, I feel like I'm going to be sick. All I can tell them, and I think this applies to many things in life, is that when you find something you dearly love, stick with it. If it's meant to be, with a little faith and luck, you'll find the right path to your goals.

After success comes, it's important to avoid resting on your laurels. Show business has seen far too many "one hit wonders." One song, no matter how much it's hyped, is not going to carry a concert if the rest of the material is crap. It's the second hit that proves you weren't a fluke, and after that there's no telling how far you can go if you maintain the right attitude.

By that, I mean that too many performers get caught up in the trappings, the hangers-on, the self-indulgent behavior. My saving grace was that lightning didn't strike for me until after I'd been around long enough to witness first hand the toll that booze, pills, and the wild life can take.

Show business can eat you alive. In 1949 I played the Earl Theater in Philadelphia. After my show they brought on stage for a promotional appearance a local boy who'd just made his first picture in Hollywood. He was born Alfredo Arnold Cocozza, but had changed his name to Mario Lanza. Soon he was a big star. Just after *Jezebel* hit it big he invited Nan and me to dinner in Beverly Hills. To my surprise, as a greeting he had copies of *Jezebel* plastered across the entryway to his house. He really loved the song! The dinner table practically sagged under succulent piles of Italian food, but all that Mario had on his plate was an apple and a tiny piece of meat. He was fighting a losing battle to keep his weight under control.

Shortly after our dinner, I dropped by one of his recording sessions with a demo of a song Carl Fischer and I had written called *When You're In Love*, which he promptly performed on his radio show. He was essentially a very nice man troubled by the pressures of his chosen profession. I had to fill in for him once on what was supposed to be his opening night at the Frontier Hotel in Las Vegas when he pulled out of the engagement because of stage fright. The last time I saw Mario was in 1957, when Nan and I ran into him in the lobby of the Hotel Excelsior in Rome. He'd moved to Italy to get away from Hollywood, but the change of scene wasn't enough. He invited us to join him for a drink, but the poor man was bloated and in a very bad way. The visit broke our hearts. Two years later, he was dead at the age of 38. What a talent, and what a terrible human tragedy.

I've said it before in this book and I'll say it again: you need a sense of perspective. I remember traveling to one engagement at the University of Denver in the late '40s.

The limo carrying Louis Jordan, Woody Herman, and me broke down and we had to get out and push. The weather was horrible, and after a few moments of sloshing around in the mire, Woody suddenly burst out laughing and leaned against the trunk. I wanted to know what the hell was so funny.

"All those worshipful kids at the school waiting to applaud and cheer their heads off," he said. "If they could see us now, boy, if they could only see us now!"

* * * * * *

It was much easier for singers to hone their craft back in the heyday of the traveling big bands and smoky little jazz clubs. Back then you could experiment in a different setting, in front of a new audience, each night. It was while making the rounds of the clubs that I picked up on *Desire*; *Shine*; *River Ste. Marie*, and so many of the other great pieces of material that served me so well when I finally got into the recording studio.

In Italy they have a marvelous substitute vehicle for promoting good songs and new talent, a forum for recognizing the contributions of singers and songwriters that I'd like to see duplicated in the United States.

In the lovely city of San Remo, on the Italian Riviera, they hold a yearly festival in which songwriters from all over Italy offer up their wares and compete with each other in several different categories. Such classics as Domenico Modugno's *Volare* have emerged from the great event, and I myself had a wonderful time participating in the festival in the mid-'60s.

In 1964 I performed two of the entries at San Remo. One was a Domenico Modugno song entitled *Che Me Importa Me* which placed seventh in the judging. The second tune was by an unknown writer named Bobby Solo. It was called *Un Lagrima Sul Viso*, and ended up coming in second. That meant that both these songs were included in the festival album that was released containing the top twelve songs. Bobby Solo later recorded *Un Lagrima Sul Viso* himself, and the record was so popular that it launched a successful career. He soon became one of Italy's top selling male vocalists.

I'd like to see San Diego become America's answer to San Remo, and I'm currently busy trying to arouse enough interest and raise the necessary funds for a similar yearly event here at home. New and established artists alike could bring their best work and have it judged by a distinguished panel of professionals who've already accomplished great things in music.

A long time ago I fell in love with what music could do for me and for those who listen to it, and it's one of my fondest hopes that one day I will see this dream become a reality. This type of event would give exposure to new talents, challenge established performers, and reward the public with some quality music. There's very likely a struggling artist performing in a bar somewhere right now with a style that could sweep the world. He or she deserves a forum.

* * * * * *

In many ways, my career came full circle with the sessions that produced the *Place in Time* album in 1985. Once again I was in my element, working with some crack jazz musicians and singing standards, like *This Can't Be Love* and *Solitude*, in much the same way I'd performed *Stardust* back in 1935 when I was singing for my supper. The joy I get from vocalizing and the spine-tingling thrill of a brilliant instrumental solo are sensations that haven't dimmed in the slightest over the intervening fifty years.

My own special place in time has afforded me a wonderful life and a long, gratifying career in music. I've collaborated with some great talents, rubbed shoulders with a few giants, and been blessed in my personal relationships. So far I've had a ball, and I have every intention of making the most that I can out of the 1990s, my seventh consecutive decade in show business.

In one of the cuts off the *Place in Time* album, I renewed my association with Michel Legrand by recording a marvelous song he'd written whose title asked the question *How Do You Keep the Music Playing?* I think I've found the answer: You do what you love best, you do it to the best of your ability, and you share the results over a lifetime with people who are dear to you.

Then with any luck, like the song says, "the music never ends . . . . .

Frankie Laine today.

APPENDIX I

A FRANKIE LAINE DISCOGRAPHY

Frankie Laine is one of the most prolific and best-selling recording artists of all time. His song catalog is comprised of hundreds of titles, and his international record sales to date have exceeded the 100,000,000 mark. Laine has 21 gold records to his credit, each of which is denoted below with a "GR."

This discography covers Laine's single and album releases from 1944 to 1992. Due to space limitations, various reissue compilations and foreign releases have been omitted. It remains a representative listing.

Serious collectors are encouraged to note the end of this listing, where the addresses of the Frankie Laine Society of America and the Frankie Laine International Appreciation Society are provided. Each of these friendly organizations have more comprehensive listings available.

THE SINGLES

Label/Record#/Title		Release Date
Gold Seal		
GS7262	In The Wee Small Hours/That's Liberty	1944
Atlas		
FL127	Melancholy Madeline/Maureen	1945
FL137	Someday Sweetheart/Baby, Baby All The Time	1945
FL141	I'm Confessin'/Heartaches	1945
FL142	Coquette/It Ain't Gonna Be Like That	1945
FL147	S'posin'/You've Changed	1945
FL148	Oh! Lady Be Good/You Can Depend On Me	1945
FL156	Moonlight in Vermont/Roses of Picardy	1945
Mercury		
3016	I May Be Wrong/(Another Artist)	1946
5003	September in the Rain/Ain't That Just Like A Woman	1946
5007 (GR)	That's My Desire/By The River Saint Marie	1946
5015	Texas & Pacific/(Another Artist)	1947
5018	Sunday Kind Of Love/Who Cares What People Say?	1947
5028	I May Be Wrong/Stay As Sweet As You Are	1947
1027 (GR)	On The Sunny Side Of The Street/Blue Turning Grey Over You	1947

1028	West End Blues/I Can't Believe You're In Love With Me	1947
1178	I'm In The Mood For Love/Cherie, I Love You	1947
1180	Rockin' Chair/Till We Meet Again	1947
5048	Mam'selle/All Of Me	1947
5059	Kiss Me Again/By The Light Of The Stars	1947
5064(GR)	Two Loves Have I/Put Yourself in My Place	1947
5091(GR)	Shine/We'll Be Together Again	1948
5096	But Beautiful/I've Only Myself to Blame	1948
5105	I'm Looking Over A Four Leaf Clover/Monday Again	1948
5114	That Ain't Right/May I Never Love Again	1948
5130	Put 'em In A Box/Baby, Don't Be Mad At Me	1948
5158	Ah, But It Happens/Hold Me	1948
5174	Singing The Blues/Thanks For You	1948
5177	You're All I Want For Christmas/Tara Talara Tala	1948
5227	Rosetta/It Only Happens Once	1949
5243	Wish You Were Jealous Of Me/Don't Have To Tell Nobody	1949
5275	September In The Rain/Sweet Talk	1949
5293	Georgia On My Mind/You're Just the Kind	1949
5301	Nevertheless/Bebop Spoken Here	1949
5311	Now That I Need You/My Own, My Only, My All	1949
5316(GR)	That Lucky Old Sun/I Get Sentimental Over Nothing	1949
5332	Waiting At The End of the Road/Don't Do Something To Somebody Else	1949
5345(GR)	Mule Train/Carry Me Back to Old Virginny	1949
5355	God Bless the Child/Don't Cry Little Children	1950
5358	Satan Wears A Satin Gown/Baby Just For Me	1950
5363(GR)	Cry of the Wild Goose/Black Lace	1950
5390(GR)	Swamp Girl/Give Me A Kiss For Tomorrow	1950
5421	Stars & Stripes Forever/Thanks For Your Kisses	1950
5442	If I Were You Baby/I Love You For That (with Patti Page)	1950
5495	Nevertheless/I Was Dancing With Someone	1950
5500	Sleepy Ol' River/If I Were A Bell	1950
5544	I'm Gonna Live Till I Die/A Man Gets Awfully Lonesome	1950
5553	Merry Christmas Everywhere/What Am I Gonna Do This Christmas?	1950

5580	May The Good Lord Bless and Keep You/Dear Dear, Dear	1951
5581	Metro Polka/The Jalopy Song	1951
5656	Heart Of My Heart/You Left Me Out In The Rain	1951
5685	Isle Of Capri/The Day Isn't Long Enough	1951
5733	Get Happy/I Would Do Most Anything For You	1951
5768	Baby I Need You/South of the Border	1951
70099	Ain't Misbehavin'/That's How Rhythm Was Born	1951

Columbia

39367(2 GRs)	Jezebel/Rose, Rose I Love You	1951
39388	Pretty-Eyed Baby/That's The One For Me (with Jo Stafford)	1951
39466	In The Cool, Cool, Cool, of the Evening/That's Good! That's Bad! (with Jo Stafford)	1952
39693	Sugarbush/How Lovely Cooks the Meat (with Doris Day)	1952
39716	Snow In Lover's Lane/That's How It Goes	1952
39770 (GR)	High Noon/Rock of Giblralter	1952
39798	Rainbow Around My Shoulder/She's Funny That Way	1952
39862	The Mermaid/The Ruby and the Pearl	1952
39867	Settin' the Woods on Fire/Piece-A-Puddin' (with Jo Stafford)	1952
39893	Chow Willy/Christmas Roses (with Jo Stafford)	1952
39903	I'm Just A Poor Bachelor/Tonight You Belong To Me	1952
39938 (2GRs)	I Believe/Your Cheatin' Heart	1953
39945	Tell Me A Story/Little Boy and the Old Man (with Jimmy Boyd)	1953
39979	Ramblin' Man/I Let Her Go	1953
40022	Where the Winds Blow/Te Amo	1953
40036	Poor Little Piggy Bank/Let's Go Fishin' (with Jimmy Boyd)	1953
40079	Answer Me O Lord/Blowing Wild	1953
40116	Way Down Yonder In New Orleans/Floating Down to Cotton Town (with Jo Stafford)	1952
40136	Granada/I'd Give My Life	1954
40178 (GR)	Kid's Last Fight/Long Distance Love	1954
40198	Goin' Like Wildfire/Rollin' Down the Line (with Jo Stafford)	1954
40235	Someday/There Must Be A Reason	1954

40295	Rain Rain, Rain/Your Heart, My Heart (with The Four Lads)	1954
40378	Old Shoes/In the Beginning'	1955
40401	High Society/Back Where I Belong (with Jo Stafford)	1955
40413	Keepin' Out Of Mischief/I Can't Give You Anything But Love	1955
40433	Bubbles/Tarrier Song	1955
40457(GR)	Cool Water/Strange Lady in Town	1955
40526	Hummingbird/My Little One	1955
40539	Mona Lisa/Laura	1955
40558	Hawkeye/Your Love	1955
40583(GR)	A Woman In Love/Walking The Night Away	1955
40600	Ain't It A Pity and a Shame/I Heard the Angels Singing (with The Four Lads)	1955
40650	Little Child/Let's Go Fishin'	1955
50006	Jezebel/Jealousy	1955
50038	High Noon/I Believe	1955
40663	Hell Hath No Fury/The Most Happy Fella	1956
40669	Moby Dick/A Capital Ship	1956
40693	Don't Cry/Ticky Ticky Tick	1956
J4-275	Robin Hood/Champion The Wonder Horse	1956
40720	Make Me A Child Again/The Thief	1956
40741	On the Road To Mandalay/Only If We Love	1956
40780(GR)	Moonlight Gambler/Lotus Land	1956
40856	Love Is a Golden Ring/There's Not A Moment To Spare	1957
40916	Gunfight At the O.K. Corral/Without Him	1957
40962	The 3:10 To Yuma/You Know How It Is	1957
40976	Good Evening Friends/Up Above My Head (with Johnny Ray)	1957
41036	The Greater Sin/East is East	1957

Mercury

30017	That Lucky Old Sun/Shine	1957
30018	Mule Train/Cry of the Wild Goose	1957
30019	That's My Desire/By the River Saint Marie	1957

Columbia

41106	Annabel Lee/All of These and More	1958
41139	My Gal and a Prayer/The Lonesome Road	1958
41163	Lovin' Up A Storm/A Kiss Can Change the World	1958
41187	Choombala Bay/I Have To Cry	1958
41230(GR)	Rawhide/Magnificent Obsession	1958

41283	Midnight On A Rainy Monday/When I Speak Your Name	1958
41331	That's My Desire/In My Wildest Dreams	1958
41376	Journey's Ended/My Little Love	1959
41430	El Diablo/Valley of a Hundred Hills	1959
41486	Rocks and Gravel/Rockin' Mother	1959
41613	St. James Infirmary/Et Voila	1960
41700	Seven Women/Doesn't She Roll	1960
41787	Here She Comes Now/Kisses That Shake The World	1961
41974	Gunslinger/Wanted Man	1961
42233	Miss Satan/Ride Through The Night	1961
3-33009	Your Cheating Heart/Jezebel	1961
42383	Wedded Man/We'll Be Together Again	1962
42767	Don't Make My Baby Blue/The Moment of Truth	1963

Mercury

30056	Georgia On My Mind/September in the Rain	1963
30062	All of Me/When You're Smiling	1963

Columbia

42884	Take Her She's Mine/I'm Gonna Be Strong	1964
42966	Up Among The Stars/Lonely Days of Winter	1964

Capitol

5299	Halfway/Go On with Your Dancing	1964
5472	House of Laughter/A Girl	1964
5525	Seven Days of Love/Heartaches Can Be Fun	1965
5569	The Meaning of It All/Pray and He Will Answer You	1966
5658	Johnny Willow/What Do You Know?	1966

ABC

10891	I'll Take Care of Your Cares/Every Street's A Boulevard	1967
10924(GR)	Making Memories/The Moment of Truth	1967
10946	You Wanted Someone To Play With/The Real True Meaning of Love	1967
10967	Laura/Sometimes I Just Can't Stand You	1967
10983	You, No One But You/Somewhere There's Someone	1967
11032	To Each His Own/I'm Happy to Hear You're Sorry	1968
11057	I Found You/I Don't Want To Set the World on Fire	1968
11097	Take Me Back/Forsaking All Others	1968
11129	Please Forgive Me/Pretty Little Princess	1968

11174(GR)	Lord, You Gave Me A Mountain/The Secret of Happiness	1969
11224	Dammit Isn't God's Last Name/Fresh Out of Tears	1969
11234	Allegra/If I Didn't Believe In You	1970
11231	I'll Take Care of Your Cares/Making Memories	1970

Amos

AJB138	I Believe/On the Sunny Side of the Street	1970
AJB153	Put Your Hand in the Hand/Going To Newport	1971
AJB161	Don't Blame the Child/My God and I	1971

Score

| SC5059 | Can You Hear Me Lord?/Going To Newport | 1972 |

Sunflower

| SNF125 | My Own True Love/Time To Ride | 1973 |

Warner Brothers

| WB7774 | Blazing Saddles/(Another Artist) | 1974 |

Mainstream

| MRL5579 | Talk To Me 'Bout the Hard Times (Parts I & II) | 1976 |

CBS

| TB16306 | If I Never Sing Another Song/We'll Be Together Again | 1981 |

Score

| FLS 201 | Take Me Back to L.A./We'll Be Together Again | 1984 |

Riclew

| RL000A | Strike Up the Band for San Diego/(Another Artist) | 1985 |

Score

| FLS 202 | San Diego, Lovely Lady By the Sea/(Another Artist) | 1985 |
| FLS 203 | Merry Christmas Without You/Old New Orleans | 1986 |

Playback

| PL1106 | Jambalaya/The Green, Green Grass of Home | 1986 |
| PL1107 | She Never Could Dance/I Believe in You | 1986 |

THE ALBUMS AND EPs
Mercury

MG25007	Frankie Laine Sings	1947
MG25026	Frankie Laine	1949
MG25025	Songs From the Heart	1949
MG25026	Frankie Laine	1949
MG25027	Frankie Laine	1949

Columbia

| CL2548 | One For My Baby (6 songs) | 1951 |
| CL6200 | One For My Baby (8 songs) | 1951 |

Mercury

MG25097	Mr. Rhythm	1952
MG25098	Song Favorites by Frankie Laine	1952
MG25124	Music Maestro Please	1952

Columbia

CL 6268	Musical Portrait of New Orleans (10 inch) (with Jo Stafford)	1953
CL578	Musical Portrait of New Orleans (12 inch) (with Jo Stafford)	1954
CL6278	Mr. Rhythm	1954
CL2504	Lover Laine	1955
CL625	Command Performance	1955
CL808	Jazz Spectacular (Re-issued in 1977 as JCL808)	1955
CL861	Frankie Laine and the Four Lads	1956

Mercury

MG20069	Songs by Frankie Laine	1956
MG20080	That's My Desire	1956
MG20083	Songs For People Together	1956
MG20085	Concert Date	1956
MG20105	With All My Heart	1956

Allegro

4132	Frankie Sings	1956

Galaxy

4821	Frankie Sings	1956

Columbia

CL975	Rockin'	1957
CL11156	Foreign Affair (with Michel Legrand)	1958
Cl1176/CS8024	Torchin'	1958

Rondolette

A-21	Frankie Laine Sings	1958

Columbia

CL1231/CS8636	Frankie Laine's Greatest Hits	1958
CL1277/CS8087	Reunion in Rhythm (with Michel Legrand, reissued in 1977 as ACS8087)	1959
CL1317/CS8119	You Are My Love	1959

Rondo

R2015/RS2015	Frankie Laine Sings/Andre Previn Plays	1959

Mercury-Wing

MW12110/SAW16110	Sings His All Time Favorites	1966
MW12202/SRW16202	That's My Desire	1960

Columbia

CL1393/CS8188	Balladeer	1960

CL1615/CS8415 Hell Bent For Leather		1961
CS8496 Deuces Wild		1962
CL1829/CS8629 Call of the Wild		1962
Mercury		
MG20578/SR60587 Frankie Laine's Golden Hits		1962
Columbia		
CL1962/CS8762 Wanderlust		1963
Harmony		
HL7329/HS11129 Roving Gambler		1964
Capitol		
T2277/ST2277 I Believe		1965
Mercury-Wing		
MR12158/SRW16158 Singing the Blues		1966
SRW16349 Frankie Laine's Greatest Hits		1967
ABC		
ABC604/ABCS604 I'll Take Care of Your Cares		1967
Harmony		
HL7425/HS11225 Frankie Laine Memories		1968
HL7382/HS11182 That's My Desire		1968
ABC		
ABC608/ABCS608 I Wanted Someone To Love		1968
ABC628/ABCS628 To Each His Own		1968
ABCS657 Take Me Back to Laine Country		1968
Tower		
T5092/TS5092 Memory Laine		1968
ABC		
ABCS682 You Gave Me A Mountain		1969
Harmony		
HS11345 I'm Gonna Live Till I Die		1969
Mercury-Wing		
PKW2-111 Frankie Laine, The Great Years		1969
Amos		
AAS-7009 Frankie Laine's Greatest Hits		1970
AAS-7013 A Brand New Day		1971
ABC		
ABCX790-2 20 Incredible Performances		1975
Springboard		
SP-4009 Frankie Laine's Greatest Hits		1975
SPX-6011 Frankie Laine Sings His Very Best		1976
ABC		
AC-30001 The ABC Collection		1976

Pickwick

SPC-3151	Heartaches Can Be Fun	1977
SPC-3526	That Lucky Old Sun	1978
SPC-3601	You Gave Me A Mountain	1979

Koala

AW14133	Frankie Laine Sings	1979

CBS-Encore

P14391	Too Marvelous For Words	1979

51 West

QR16047	Pick of Frankie Laine	1979

Exact

Ex-242	Frankie Laine's Best	1981

CBS

P-15166	Now and Then	1981

Hindsight

HSR198	The Uncollected Frankie Laine-1947	1984
HSR216	The Uncollected, Volume 2	1985

Score

FLP 101	So Ultra Rare	1984
FLP 102	Frankie Laine's Place In Time	1985

Jubilate

J1506	Frankie's Gold	1985

Playback

PP1 12004	A Country Laine	1986

Score

FLC-2002	New Directions	1988

Score

FLC-2005	Riders in the Sky	1991

SELECTED COMPACT DISCS:

Telarc

CD-80141	Round-Up, with Eric Kunzel and the Cincinnati Pops Orchestra	1987

Columbia

CK 45029	Frankie Laine: 16 Most Requested Songs	1989

Bear Family

BCD 15480	Frankie Laine — On the Trail	1990

Polygram

314 510 435-2	The Frankie Laine Collection — The Mercury Years	1991

Score

FLCD 0691	Frankie Laine and Friends (A Collection of Duets)	1991

FLCD 0691 Frankie Laine and Friends (A Collection of Duets)1991
FOREIGN RELEASES
   (NOTE: Frankie Laine's tremendous international success is reflected in the fact that his American releases have been repackaged
and reissued countless times in Canada, Britain, Italy, France, Germany, South Africa, South America, Japan, Australia and elsewhere
abroad. A full accounting of these records, not to mention an attempt to catalog the myriad bootlegs which have surfaced over the
years, lies outside the scope of this discography. Instead, listed
below are several titles which were either specifically recorded for a
foreign market, or were originally compiled in that country.)

BRITAIN:
Polydor
2383-457	20 Memories in Gold	1977
2383-488	Life is Beautiful	1978

Bulldog
BDL 1035	All Of Me (early period Laine compilation)	1984

World RecordClub
SM 531-6	The Frankie Laine Songbook (6 album set)	1979

Castle
CD CST 43	Frankie Laine — The Country Store Collection (compact disc)	1989

Harmony
HARCD 102	Frankie Laine — Portrait of a Song Stylist (compact disc)	1989

Prestige
PRCDSP300	Somethin' Old, Somethin' New (compact disc)	1992

HOLLAND:
Arcade
ADEH 91	The World of Frankie Laine	1982

   (NOTE: This album, a twenty track selection of newly recorded versions of Laine's greatest hits, was recorded in Nashville for the Holland-based Arcade record label. It became a
number-one seller in Holland and was certified gold shortly after its
release.)

* * * * * *

For further information on Frankie Laine and his activities, please contact his American or International Appreciation Societies. These groups are dedicated to the propagation of Laine and his music, and they will be happy to hear from you.

The Frankie Laine Society of America
14322 Califa Street
Van Nuys, California 91401

The Frankie Laine International Appreciation Society
Silsden Cottage, Amersham Road
Chalfont St. Giles, Bucks HP8 4ND
England.

APPENDIX II

FILM, TELEVISION, AND RADIO PERFORMANCES

FILMS

From the early to mid-1950s, Frankie Laine starred in a series of five motion pictures for Columbia Studios. These films were pleasant (albeit lightweight) musical entertainments which occasionally featured performers like Billy Daniels, Bob Crosby, and Kay Starr in supporting roles.

Though they do not constitute a major phase of his career, the movies did at least provide Laine's admirers in Europe and elsewhere abroad with their first opportunity to see him in action.

It is also interesting to note that one of the films, **Bring Your Smile Along**, marked the directorial debut of Blake Edwards.

Following each title below is a listing of the songs performed by Laine in the film:

When You're Smiling — 1950. *When You're Smiling; Georgia On My Mind.*

Sunny Side of the Street — 1951. *Pennies From Heaven; On the Sunny Side of the Street; I May Be Wrong; I'm Gonna Live 'Till I Die.*

Rainbow 'Round My Shoulder — 1952. *Wrap Your Troubles in Dreams; The Girl in the Wood; Wonderful, Wasn't It?; There's A Rainbow 'Round My Shoulder; Ain't Misbehavin'.*

Bring Your Smile Along — 1955. *Bring Your Smile Along; If Spring Never Comes; Mama Mia; Side by Side; When A Girl Is Beautiful; The Gandy Dancer's Ball.*

He Laughed Last — *1956. Danny Boy; Save Your Sorrow For Tomorrow.*

In addition to these films, Frankie Laine made brief appearances in the following two motion pictures:

Make Believe Ballroom — Columbia, 1949. In this montage of musical performances based on the radio programs of Al Jarvis and Martin Block, Laine is featured singing *On the Sunny Side of the Street.*

Meet Me in Las Vegas — MGM, 1956. In this musical starring Cyd Charisse and Dan Dailey, Laine is seen singing *Hell Hath No Fury.*

Frankie Laine has performed the title song for the following motion pictures:

Blowing Wild — Warner, 1953.

A Man Without A Star — Universal, 1955.
Strange Lady In Town — Warner, 1955.
Gunfight at the O.K. Corral — Paramount, 1957.
The 3:10 To Yuma — Columbia, 1957.
Bullwhip — Republic, 1958.
Blazing Saddles — Warner/Crossbow, 1974.

Laine's music is also featured at some point in the soundtrack of:
The Last Picture Show — Columbia, 1971. *Rose, Rose I Love You*
All This and World War II — Deluxe, 1977. *Maxwell's Silver Hammer*
Lemon Popsicle — 1978. *My Little One*
Going Steady — 1980. *My Little One*
House Calls — Universal, 1978. *On the Sunny Side of the Street*
Raging Bull — United Artists,1980. *That's My Desire*
Whore - 1991. *Love of Loves*

TELEVISION

Frankie Laine Time — In the early 1950s, Frankie Laine filmed a series of fifteen-minute television programs for Guild Films in London. These were widely syndicated in the U.S., and frequently featured European vaudeville acts. Singer Connie Haines often acted as Laine's co-hostess. When the fifteen-minute format faded from use, two shows were combined to fill half-hour time slots. This program was originally sponsored by Hamm's Beer.

The Frankie Laine Show — CBS, Wednesdays, 8-9 pm, 1955-1956 — Beginning as a summer replacement series for **Arthur Godfrey and His Friends,** this musical variety program featured Laine singing and performing in comedy skits with his various guests.

Frankie Laine has been a featured guest on many talk shows and variety programs, far too numerous to recount here. What follows is instead a listing of some of his dramatic performances and other guest appearances of special note:

Perry Mason - CBS, 1957-1966. Laine attempted his first dramatic television role, to excellent reviews, playing a bigtime comic down on his luck in a 1959 episode entitled *The Case of the Jaded Joker*.

Rawhide — CBS, 1959-1966. In a 1960 episode of this long-running Western series (which featured Laine's stirring rendition of its theme song every week) entitled *Incident on the Road to Yesterday*, Frankie Laine was given the special opportunity to play opposite his wife Nan in a love story. Nan Grey left the screen upon becoming Mrs. Laine, and this special appearance marked the former Universal starlet's brief return to acting after nearly two decades away.

Burke's Law — ABC, 1963-1966. Laine guest starred as a villainous corporate lawyer in *Who Killed Wade Walker?*, an episode from the first season of this crime series.

The Nat King Cole Show — NBC, 1956-1957. It should be noted that Frankie Laine was the first white performer to cross the "color line" and guest star on the black vocalist's musical series (a sustaining program which failed to secure a regular sponsor). Many others followed Laine onto the program but all their efforts, not to mention the prodigious talents of Cole himself, were insufficient to save the program from the racial intolerance of that era.

In addition to his dramatic roles, Laine also guested on two situation comedies: **The Danny Thomas Show** *(Make Room For Daddy)* — ABC, 1953-1957; and **Bachelor Father** — CBS, 1957-1959.

Frankie Laine performed the theme songs for the following television series:

Gunslinger — CBS, 1961
The Misadventures of Sheriff Lobo (1st Season) — NBC, 1979-1981
Rango — ABC, 1967
Rawhide — CBS, 1959-1966

RADIO

Although Frankie Laine's surge to national prominence did not occur until the Golden Age of Radio was drawing to a close, this medium nonetheless occupied a portion of his time in the late 1940s and early 1950s.

Some of his early broadcast performances as part of Al Jarvis's **Make Believe Ballroom Four** were transcribed and later commercially released in the United States and Europe on the Rondolette and Ember record labels (see Appendix I).

Soon after *That's My Desire* gained him national recognition in 1947, several appearances on **The Chesterfield Supper Club** helped to further showcase Laine's talents. He later guested on **The Big Show**, an NBC radio extravaganza hosted by Tallulah Bankhead that constituted the medium's last defiant gesture against the onslaught of television.

A November 26, 1947 broadcast of **Philco Radio Time** is worth noting for the opportunity it provided Laine to exchange banter with its genial host, one of his early singing idols, Bing Crosby.

In the early 1950s, Laine was briefly featured on two series of U.S. Government sponsored programs, one for the U.S. Treasury Department and the other on behalf of the Army.

APPENDIX III

SONGWRITING

Few people are aware of Frankie Laine's "second calling." Although he will always be thought of chiefly as an important and influential vocalist, he has also turned his attention, with considerable success, to the art of writing songs.

Over the years Laine's collaborators have included such notables as Hoagy Carmichael (*Put Yourself In My Place, Baby*), Mel Tormé (*It Ain't Gonna Be Like That*), Duke Ellington (*What Am I Here For?*), and Matt Dennis (*Allegra*). In 1958, with his then current accompanist Al Lerner, Laine penned the title track to his Columbia LP, *Torchin'*.

Laine is particularly proud of *Magnificent Obsession* (written with Freddy Karger) and his many collaborations with the late Carl Fischer. Foremost among the latter, of course, is *We'll Be Together Again*, a classic evergreen that has been recorded by well over 100 different artists.

The lyrics to this lovely standard are reprinted below, followed by a selected alphabetical listing of some of its notable performances as well as a few other interesting entries from Laine's catalog, with each song followed by a comment from Laine :

We'll Be Together Again

(Lyrics by Frankie Laine; Music by Carl Fischer; Copyright 1945, Cares Music, Los Angeles)

> *Here in our moment of darkness*
> *Remember the sun has shown*
> *Laugh and the world will laugh with you*
> *Cry and you cry alone*
>
> *No tears, no fears*
> *Remember there's always tomorrow*
> *So what if we have to part*
> *We'll be together again*
>
> *Your kiss, your smile*
> *Are mem'ries I'll treasure forever*
> *So try thinking with your heart*
> *We'll be together again*

Times when I know you'll be lonesome
Times when I know you'll be sad
Don't let temptation surround you
Don't let the blues make you bad

Some day, some way
We both have a lifetime before us
For parting is not goodbye
We'll be together again.

Selected Performances:

Artist/Label

Louis Armstrong/MGM
Tony Bennett-Bill Evans/Fantasy
Les Brown-Doris Day/Columbia
Ruth Brown/Atlantic
Ray Charles-Betty Carter/ABC
Kenny Clarke/Savoy
Rosemary Clooney/Columbia
Sammy Davis, Jr./Reprise
Ella Fitzgerald/Verve
The Four Freshmen/Capitol
Stan Getz/Verve
The Chico Hamilton Trio/Pacific Jazz
Billie Holiday/Verve
J.J. Johnson-Kai Winding/Prestige
Jack Jones/EMI
Quincy Jones/ABC
Stan Kenton/Capitol
Mark Murphy/Muse
Carmen McRae/Decca
Red Norvo/Stash
Anita O'Day/Verve
The Joe Pass Trio/Pablo
Oscar Peterson/Verve
The Pied Pipers/Capitol
George Shearing/MGM
Horace Silver/Blue Note
Frank Sinatra/Capitol
Ben Webster/Verve
Dianne Schurr/Atlantic

IT ONLY HAPPENS ONCE

(Music and Lyrics: Frankie Laine)

It only happens once
I'll never feel that thrill again
It only happens once
Why couldn't I have known it then
Since I lost you dear one
Nothing seems to be the same
I try hard but it's no use
My heart won't play the game
It only happens once
I realize it now it's past
And I was such a dunce
'Cause I couldn't make it last
So why go on pretending
I just can't love someone new
It only happens once
And for me that once was you

* * * * * *

COMMENT: This was the first song I ever wrote. I'm only sorry that more people haven't had a chance to hear the great transcription recording that Nat King Cole made of this song. He did a beautiful job.

PUT YOURSELF IN MY PLACE BABY

(Music and Lyrics: Laine and Hoagy Carmichael)

Put yourself in my place Baby
And try to understand the way I feel
Imagine the tables turned and how I've yearned
To have you back in my arms
Wouldn't that be Heaven

Put yourself in my place Baby
Remember it's my first affair
Those moments that we knew so well
Deserve another try
Two people with the same sweet memories
Shouldn't let love go by

Put yourself in my place Baby
Then you'll know how much I really care
Just think about it twice, it's easy to be nice
Baby put yourself in my place

* * * * * *

It took a while after *Desire* caught fire before I was able to get back together with Hoagy Carmichael and thank him for his role in my success. We collaborated on this song, which I recorded while at Mercury. They issued it as the flip side of *Two Loves Have I*.

IT AIN'T GONNA BE LIKE THAT

(Music and Lyrics: Laine and Mel Tormé)

You better button your lip
You better watch what you do.
'Cause the days of your miserable ways are through
It ain't gonna be like that

If you think you can wind me around your finger
Best get your coat and your hat
'Cause it ain't gonna be like that

If you think that you can put me through the wringer
There'll be the devil to pay
'Cause it ain't gonna be that way
There ain't no gal in the whole wide world
Who can ever be my boss
Better take it slow or I'm gonna throw you for a total loss
Gonna be no welcome mat
If you're gonna bring me down please don't linger
Baby, I'm standing pat
Cause it ain't gonna be like that

* * * * * *

Mel dropped by my office one afternoon in the late '40s, and during the course of our conversation he responded to a question of mine by saying, "It ain't gonna be like that!" We were both so taken with the phrase that we put our heads together and worked out this song in no time.

218

I HAVEN'T THE HEART

(Music and Lyrics: Laine and Matt Dennis)

> *I haven't the heart to fall in love again*
> *For though you say we're through*
> *I'm still in love with you, I'm yours*
> *And I haven't the heart to give to someone else*
> *I know because I've tried*
> *Still way down deep inside I'm yours*
> *At night I dream about your face*
> *The touch of your hand*
> *The thrill of your warm embrace*
> *I haven't the heart to care for someone new*
> *Why should I even try*
> *When I know that I'm still yours*
> *When I know I'm yours*

* * * * * *

It was a real pleasure to work with Matt Dennis, an extremely talented gentleman who's provided the music for such all-time classics as *The Night We Called It A Day*, *Angel Eyes*, and *Violets For Your Furs*. Many years after we wrote this song in the '40s, we collaborated on a ballad entitled *Allegra* which appeared on the *You Gave Me A Mountain* album.

MAGNIFICENT OBSESSION

(Music and Lyrics: Laine and Fred Karger)

> *As long as I have breath within me*
> *You'll be my one and only love*
> *You're my magnificent obsession*
> *The greatest wonder on this earth*
> *The Taj Mahal and other splendors*
> *To me really have no worth*
> *You're my magnificent possession*
> *A treasure leant me from above*
> *As long as I have breath within me*
> *You'll be my one and only love*
>
> *You're my magnificent possession*
> *A treasure leant me from above*
> *As long as I have breath within me*
> *You'll be my one and only love*

* * * * * *

I'm really very proud of this song, and consider it to be one of my best. I'm still absolutely floored every time I listen to the great job Nat King Cole did with it.

TORCHIN'

(Music and Lyrics: Laine and Al Lerner)

I sit alone just crying
Remembering the laughs and tears
The happiness through the years
The love I thought would last

Broken hearted I hear a ghostly love theme
That you used to sing for me
My heart is in agony
For dreams are ever past

So many tender memories
Of all that used to be
That made life so sublime
But now what good are reveries
That only torture me
And make a torment of time

And here I sit alone just praying
Some miracle brings your heart
Back into this world apart
Where I will stay
Hoping you will find your way to me again

* * * * * *

This is a torch song about torch songs! It served as the title track of a 1958 Columbia album full of barroom weepers and mood music for those early morning hours.

I'D GIVE MY LIFE

(Music and Lyrics: Laine and Carl Fischer)

I'd give my life to have your love
I have no life without your love
I have no stars in the sky, no moon to see
There are no birds that will sing for me
Your eyes are beautiful to see
Your lips would bring such ecstasy
So till the day you are mine
I swear by all that's above
I'd give my life to have your love

* * * * * *

This is just one of many, many pieces I collaborated on with my best friend and musical soul mate, the late Carl Fischer. We were both interested in a wide variety of music, and I remember that we based the opening of this song on an old German leider.

ONLY IF WE LOVE

(Music and Lyrics: Laine and Al Lerner)

Only if we love will there be starlight
Shining on a starless night
Only if we care will there be blossoms
Shimmering on a tree you know is bare
Only if we give our hearts to someone
Will we truly start to live
Only if we share our dreams
Will someone come to build our castles in the air

Wonders of spring for all time
Are in your innermost soul
And nevermore will there be a fall time
At last your heart has reached its goal
This is why my love I must have just you
Only love makes life anew
Only love just me then there's heaven on earth
A treasure rare so rich in worth
And it cannot be measured
But only if you love just me

* * * * * *

I'm particularly fond of this lyric for its poetic quality. I've always believed that good songwriting is poetry set to music, and that a lyric crafted with sensitivity can help unlock some of the hidden delights amongst the notes.

INDEX

224

227

ORDER FORM

Pathfinder Publishing of California
458 Dorothy Ave.
Ventura, CA 93003
Telephone (805) 642-9278   FAX (805) 650-3656

Please send me the following books from Pathfinder Publishing:

_____ Copies of **Dialogues In Swing** @ $12.95 $_____

More Dialogues In Swing
_____ Copies--Softcover @ $14.95 $_____
_____ Copies--Hardcover @ $22.95 $_____

That Lucky Old Son
_____ Copies--Softcover @ $14.95 $_____
_____ Copies--Hardcover @ $21.95 $_____

_____ Copies of **World of Gene Krupa** @ $14.95 $_____

                       Sub-Total $_____
Californians: Please add 7.25% tax. $_____
Shipping* $_____
                       Grand Total $_____

I understand that I may return the book for a full refund if not satisfied.
Name:_____

Address:_____
_____ZIP:_____

*SHIPPING CHARGES U.S.
Books: Enclose $2.50 for the first book and .50c for each additional book. UPS: Truck; $4.00 for first item, .50c for each additional. UPS Air: $7.50 for first item, $.75 for each additional item.